Visualising Facebook

WHY WE POST

PUBLISHED AND FORTHCOMING TITLES:

Download free: www.ucl.ac.uk/ucl-press

**Why
We
Post**

Visualising Facebook

A Comparative Perspective

Daniel Miller and Jolynna Sinanan

First published in 2017 by
UCL Press
University College London
Gower Street
London WC1E 6BT

Available to download free: www.ucl.ac.uk/ucl-press

A CIP catalogue record for this book is available
from The British Library.

ISBN: 978–1–911307–35–8 (Hbk.)
ISBN: 978–1–911307–36–5 (Pbk.)
ISBN: 978–1–911307–40–2 (PDF)
ISBN: 978–1–911307–39–6 (epub)
ISBN: 978–1–911307–38–9 (mobi)
ISBN: 978–1–911307–37–2 (html)
DOI: https://doi.org/10.14324/111.9781911307402

Introduction to the series Why We Post

This book is one of a series of 11 titles. Nine are monographs devoted to specific field sites in Brazil, Chile, China, England, India, Italy, Trinidad and Turkey. The series also includes a comparative book about all our findings, published to accompany this title.

When we tell people that we have written nine monographs about social media around the world, and that they all have the same chapter headings (apart from Chapter 5), they are concerned about potential repetition. However, if you decide to read several of these books (and we very much hope you do), you will see that this device has been helpful in showing the precise opposite. Each book is as individual and distinct as if it were on an entirely different topic.

This is perhaps our single most important finding. Most studies of the internet and social media are based on research methods that assume we can generalise across different groups. We look at tweets in one place and write about 'Twitter'. We conduct tests about social media and friendship in one population, and then write on this topic as if friendship means the same thing for all populations. By presenting nine books with the same chapter headings, you can judge for yourselves what kinds of generalisations are, or are not, possible.

Our intention is not to evaluate social media, either positively or negatively. Instead the purpose is educational, providing detailed evidence of what social media has become in each place and the local consequences, including local evaluations.

Each book is based on 15 months of research during which time the anthropologists lived, worked and interacted with people in the local language. Yet they differ from the dominant tradition of writing social science books. Firstly, they do not engage with the academic literatures on social media. It would be highly repetitive to have the same discussions in all nine books. Instead discussions of these literatures are to be found in our comparative book, *How the World Changed Social Media*. Secondly, these monographs are not comparative, which again is the primary function of this other volume. Thirdly, given the immense interest in social media from the general public, we have tried to write in an accessible and open style. This means we have adopted a mode more common in historical writing of keeping all citations and the discussion of all wider academic issues to endnotes. If you prefer to read above the line, each text offers a simple narrative about our findings. If you want to read a more conventional academic book that relates the material to its academic context, this can be done through engaging with the footnotes. We hope you enjoy the results and that you will also read our comparative book – and perhaps some of the other monographs – in addition to this one.

Visualising Facebook stands out from the crowd. It is neither a comparison of all the sites nor an individual monograph. Instead this book allows us to focus upon a more systematic comparison of the images people post in two of our field sites. The sheer number of images included within this volume make it a slightly different contribution from the others within the series, to the degree that you can literally 'see' what we are talking about when we argue for cultural difference.

Acknowledgements

It is in the nature of anthropological research that we cannot name directly those to whom we owe our greatest debt. These are the people of El Mirador and The Glades who gave us their time, often friendship, trust, access to their private worlds and consent forms, without which this publication would not have been possible. We hope they will feel that this work does indeed help people around the world to appreciate and understand each others' societies and contribute to the project of anthropology, which is the claim we made. Daniel Miller would like to thank Ciara Green who was his co-worker throughout the ethnography of The Glades.

All our research has been carried out as two of the nine team members of the 'Why We Post' project, and this book was written in constant dialogue and with extensive comments from Elisabetta Costa, Nell Haynes, Tom McDonald, Razvan Nicolescu, Juliano Spyer, Shriram Venkatraman and Xinyuan Wang. We also had comments on the draft manuscript from Inge Daniels and Sheba Mohammid, Justin Bourke, Pilar Lacasa, Saffiyya Mohammed and Shireen Walton, and from the anonymous readers selected by our publisher. We are very grateful for the detailed edit conducted by Laura Haapio-Kirk, who created illustrations for Chapters 4, 6 and 8.

We would also like to thank the European Research Council for funding this research – grant ERC-2011-AdG-295486 Socnet.

Contents

1
Introduction

This book has three main aims which are surprising only in terms of how little has been done previously to fulfil them. In 2011 Miller published a book called *Tales From Facebook*.[1] As the title suggests, that book consisted mainly of stories about how people, as it happens people in Trinidad, used Facebook, and the consequences of Facebook for their lives.

In retrospect there were (at least) two glaring omissions from that book. The first is that there was not one single visual image – *Tales from Facebook* contained relatively few examples of postings and these were all textual. Yet it was already evident that in places such as Trinidad the dominant form of posting on Facebook is actually visual. The book was not alone in this omission. There are several journals devoted to internet studies, and increasingly these are focused upon social media. Yet one can browse through a whole issue about new media and society or about computer-mediated communication and not find one single illustration of a visual posting. We know of no precedent that even looks like this book.

The primary reason for this has been cost, with publishers either refusing to publish colour images or charging authors considerable amounts in order to do so. But today, as shown by this volume, this is no longer the case and it is important that academics seize this new opportunity. It is surely 'about time' that a book is produced which is not only dedicated to the acknowledgement and discussion of such visuals, but also based on the reproduction of those same images that make up so much of what is posted online. Indeed one of the core arguments of our wider 'Why We Post' comparative project is that social media has transformed human communication precisely by making images as much a part of human communication as text or speech.[2] The second omission was that while *Tales From Facebook* was written about Trinidad, it did not claim that Trinidad was in and of itself any more important or interesting than any other place. Trinidad was used merely to demonstrate through a case study that Facebook is culturally specific, and is always encountered with respect to some particular population. This was a deliberate provocation in the face of hundreds of journal articles whose premise seems to be that there is a single thing called Facebook, and that if one conducts an experiment on some aspect of how people post among, for example, American college students, an academic paper can then extrapolate from that to a thing called 'Facebook' in general. Many of these same journals use methods which aim to emulate the natural sciences in the way they generalise from a case study to the universal, which makes cultural diversity something of an inconvenience.

Popular criticism of *Tales From Facebook,* including reviews on web-sites such as Amazon, indicated that the book made people uncomfortable. They suggested that a book 'about Trinidad' was quite unsuitable for the purpose of exemplifying this thing called Facebook. Yet had that book been about the use of Facebook in the US or the UK, hardly anyone would have worried about the claims being made. Our second aim is to take this point further. The argument that one simply cannot ignore such cultural diversity becomes much stronger if, instead of a single case study, we make a direct comparison between two different populations. Again what is strange is how rare such an obvious strategy seems to be.

A third aim comes more from a specific curiosity of anthropology. We wanted to know whether we could write something akin to an ethnography – that is, a portrait of a place and its population composed through the broad brushstrokes of observable and generalised cultural norms. In this instance, critically, the ethnography would be based largely upon the images people post on Facebook. This differs from our usual mode of general participation and observation which, while including online behaviour, emphasises the importance of the wider offline context required to account for this online activity. If such an ethnography were possible, how would the result compare to the kinds of writing that emerge from more conventional versions?

It is perhaps not an entirely fair comparison since we have previously written such ethnographies. In the case of Trinidad, Sinanan is completing an individual volume about social media in El Mirador as part of the 'Why We Post' series, based on her ethnographic field work in Trinidad.[3] Miller has published a general ethnography about the island too, and both authors have also written together a book called *Webcam* which is based on the same field site as this book,[4] referred to as El Mirador.[5] Miller also recently published a book about The Glades,[6] his English village field site, though the focus is on social media rather than a general ethnography. The nearest equivalent in terms of an attempt generally to characterise Englishness is probably Kate Fox's *Watching the English*;[7] based on areas such as Oxfordshire, it also broadly represents southeast England.

Although our perspective comes from anthropology, we would hope that these three aims are of interest to pretty much anyone. Who wouldn't want to know more about the consequences of this rise in the use of images within communication, the implications of cultural diversity and whether we can understand more about a population based largely upon its visual culture? The third task has some precedent in art history, but the difference is the sheer quantity of images being shared on social media and the fact that a very significant proportion of the population participates in creating them.

Given this level of general interest, we feel it would be a great pity if this book was read only by people studying a single discipline for purposes such as an academic examination. So we have tried to write in a generally clear and accessible style, wherever possible using colloquial language. There is a brief discussion of the academic foundations at the end of this chapter, while what we regard as essential references appear in endnotes elsewhere in the book. We have tried to keep these to a minimum, however, and to concentrate on our own original findings and the evidence behind our arguments. In the section on methodology, we explain how we employed quantitative as well as qualitative methods and examined over 20,000 images to try and ensure that the requisite level of scholarship underlies our arguments and conclusions.

The Glades and El Mirador

All images reproduced in this volume come from the social media postings of people who live in one of two locations: The Glades in southeast England and El Mirador in East Trinidad. Both of these names are pseudonyms. During 2012–14 Sinanan lived for 15 months in El Mirador for this particular study, while Miller spent 18 months working in The Glades on an almost daily basis. Sinanan and to a lesser extent Miller had also spent many months in El Mirador on previous projects, including the field work that led to the joint publication *Webcam*.

The two villages that make up The Glades consist of Leeglade, with around 11,000 inhabitants, and Highglade with around 6,500. Once an entirely rural site, its proximity to London led to the development of local industry in the nineteenth century. Most of this has now disappeared apart from a small commercial estate. Today the population includes commuters, who take advantage of train links that reach central London in less than an hour. More people are involved in the building trades, for instance as plumbers and electricians; they also benefit from the good road links. But although The Glades thereby represent a new kind of suburban ideal, enabling people to live in a village surrounded by fields but also have access to metropolitan London. Yet the people who live there would insist that these are villages.

Despite the proximity to one of the most cosmopolitan cities in the world, Leeglade and Highglade are homogeneously white English. The entire Afro-Caribbean, African, mixed and Asian populations only amount to two per cent of the total,[8] and the presence of Eastern European migrants is also very slight. It is also homogeneously middle class, though the presence of social housing and low income villagers is discussed in Chapter 4. Highglade in particular is fairly affluent and almost crime-free – characteristic of what in England is called 'the home counties'. So although this had not been the original intention, Miller soon realised that this was an unusual opportunity to study an iconic version of 'Englishness'. As a result this is a very specific kind of English society which despite its proximity to London has actually very little in common with the metropolitan region. We would thus not wish to generalise from this particular study to other areas of England such as London or rural areas in the North and West.

El Mirador is a small town in Trinidad, the larger island of the state of Trinidad and Tobago. Trinidad and Tobago is a Caribbean country just off the coast of northeast Venezuela with a population of around 1,200,000. Just over one-third of these are the descendants of enslaved Africans. A similar proportion are descendants from indentured East Indians from South Asia. The rest would be mixed and 'other'. El Mirador itself has around 18,000 inhabitants, perhaps 25,000 if one includes squatters on the periphery, and is located in the poorest region of the island.

Though today El Mirador is reasonably well equipped with a hospital, schools and government facilities, it is still regarded by most Trinidadians as something of a backwater. The people who live there look to the capital city of Port of Spain as their metropolitan centre, which can be reached within a couple of hours. By contrast, for the smaller villages in the hinterland El Mirador represents a local centre. It attracts them because of its bustling market, high street shopping and modest degree of entertainment – mainly consisting of bars and some live music. Of critical importance is that El Mirador has a Kentucky Fried Chicken (and local rivals), which in Trinidad is what differentiates a proper town from any other settlement.

Methodology and ethics

The primary method employed was ethnography. Some people dismiss qualitative work as merely 'anecdotal', but one can collect anecdotes in a couple of weeks. By contrast we spent 15 months in El Mirador and 18 months in The Glades, trying to ensure that we could speak with some confidence in general terms about these populations. The discussions reported in this book are about people who in almost every case we know – as a result, we also know more about them than appears in their photos. We are simultaneously writing more general books about their use of social media and indeed about these societies.[9] So the online material can always be considered in the light of our offline knowledge. Knowing about people's friends, beliefs, families and other interests is essential to understanding why they post particular images. However in this book, in addition, we look for patterns that emerge around the study of images in their own right.

With respect to identifying larger patterns of posting, our main approach was simply to stare at thousands of visual postings and try and identify repetition and genres. Every image produced here is a claim to some kind of typicality, unless it is noted as exceptional. To demonstrate this claim to being representative, we also undertook a quantitative analysis whose details and results are found in the Appendix. This included a survey of the last 300 images posted by each of 100 informants; 50 from each site, as well as a study of their 20 most recent postings and a more specific study of both their profile pictures and their selfies. Results from this Appendix are discussed throughout the book. In particular, these surveys indicate in which areas postings in El Mirador and The Glades seem similar in content and quantity and those in which we can identify clear contrasts.

The survey, and indeed virtually all the content of this book, is limited to Facebook. This would be a reasonable strategy for El Mirador since at the time of research Sinanan was following 271 informants on Facebook, but found very little usage of Twitter and only some initial interest in Instagram. By contrast, Miller followed 130 informants on Facebook, 80 on Twitter and 55 on Instagram, since younger people in The Glades made considerable use of these other platforms. Since the purpose of this volume is direct comparison, however, we decided to discuss mainly Facebook here. A discussion of both Twitter and Instagram postings has been published elsewhere.[10] This inevitably creates a degree of distortion, since some of what people in El Mirador do on Facebook, young people in The Glades now do on Instagram and Twitter. By the time of our field work Facebook was becoming considered uncool by young people in The Glades, but they all used it and retained images from a time when it was their primary platform.

Terms such as 'qualitative' and 'quantitative' are not simple distinctions. A category of image analysis such as 'are they smiling?' or 'are they trying to look hot?' or even 'is this a selfie?' implies that a qualitative judgement underlies the quantitative count. Unless it is taken in front of a mirror, you simply can't be sure this is a selfie (a self-taken image) even if the subject's arm is outstretched in front of him or her. This is also why we have one chapter, Chapter 8, that stands out from the others. We are concerned not to claim any simple objectivity to our interpretations of these visual images. Nor do we assume this should be based solely on the photographer's intention, because this does not determine the consequence of an image for the viewer. In Chapter 8 we examine how 10 different people respond to the same set of images, precisely in order to demonstrate how radically these may differ from that intention and from each other, and to explore how easily people change their opinions about what they are seeing.

Then again, who are these 'people'? There is no homogeneous group called 'the people of El Mirador'. The meaning of images may be interpreted differently by those from different classes or genders. By the same token, The Glades is not England and El Mirador is not Trinidad. Technically, every time we use the term 'English' you should assume the caveat: 'English – only as represented by the specific case of The Glades and in turn subject to every level of differentiation down to the diversity of each individual that lives in The Glades.' But having noted this here, it would be very tedious to repeat it throughout. Furthermore, comparing genres between the two sites shows why it is also important to acknowledge generalities and typicality.

Finally the reader will note that the images included in this text represent a spectrum from those that remain unaltered to those that are somewhat blurred to those that are heavily disguised, which may be sometimes distracting. We apologise for this, a reflection of ethical issues in the reproduction of other people's photographs. In general, where we have clear consent from the individual to post the original image this remains unaltered. Where people appear as background, or we do not know who these people are, then we have blurred the image so that other people will not recognise them. Where the image has been criticised by others, as in Chapter 8, or where we feel there is any possibility that harm could arise from recognition, which is our primary ethical concern, then we have replaced the individuals in the photos with illustrations which depict the same poses but with altered facial features, to such an extent that even the subjects would not recognise themselves. Differences in blurring also reflect cultural differences. We found English people to have very strong concerns over particular kinds of privacy that are different from those encountered in Trinidad. For example, the blurring of babies' faces so they cannot be identified. The result is inevitably a rather messy mix of our own concern to anonymise in order not to cause harm and our informants' quite variable sensibilities around this issue.

Academic studies

If this were a book about conventional photography then it would be reasonable to expect an extended discussion of past academic writings on that subject. Many iconic figures, such as Benjamin, Barthes and Sontag,[11] among others, have written brilliantly on the historical impact of photography in relation to topics such as memory and history, representation and truth. Anthropologists and other social scientists have, since the time of Bateson and Mead in the 1930s,[12] experimented with the interplay between photography and text in presenting ethnography and discussed the problematic relationship between the two.[13] There certainly are volumes that are replete with photographic images.[14]

While this book is about photographs, however, it is only concerned with images posted on social media – images that may be widely circulated memes as well as personal photographs. As a result, it is not at all obvious how the content of this book might be related to those prior discussions. We have not assumed that images on social media are the same kind of material as traditional genres of photography. Yet neither have we assumed that there is such a radical break between traditional analogue photographs and these images that the former have become irrelevant or incommensurate with the latter.

Actually photography has always been dynamic, reinventing itself in various respects over the decades. As a result there are bound to be a mixture of breaks and continuities. Some of these established debates clearly pertain more to historical precedents than to the material discussed here. Social media photography is a long way from an earlier connection between photography and high art. The trajectory from elite usage through to what Bourdieu called a middle-brow profession[15] has now ended in an ubiquitous presence available to low income populations. There has, however, always been an ambiguous area between photography as a profession and a hobby[16], and today an interest in Flickr or even Instagram can indicate the degree to which a person feels serious about their photography.

There are many debates about the relationship between analogue and digital photography. For example, a recent claim by Sarvas and Frohlich for digital photography expresses the view 'that communication has surpassed memory as the primary function of domestic photography, and that identity is now fighting for second place.'[17] This has been recently contested by Keightley and Pickering, however, who want to lay stress on continuities.[18] Other accounts try to determine how far digital photography remains a form of social memory comparable with the prior use of analogue photography.[19] Anthropologists have also become engaged with many aspects of the new digital photography.[20] Such discussions are of considerable interest and importance. They are not part of the brief for this particular book simply because the topic is not really an attempt to understand the nature of social media photography per se, but rather to employ this material as a new medium for the study and expression of cultural difference.

We start with the acknowledgement that there have always been a multitude of different 'photographies'. So this book might hint that older female Trinidadians relate to the genre of Carnival photographs in ways that correspond to their traditional offline engagement, or that elderly people from The Glades make holiday photos into albums for Facebook much as they did in the past. We may recognise that genres of photography such as wedding albums in both sites go back to the 1880s, so historical factors may still influence their incorporation within social media. Mostly, however, this book is a lesson in why we need to be cautious when talking about a generalised object called 'photography'. Rather the emphasis is on difference, revealing how a genre of photography, even a new one such as the selfie, may be quite different in England compared with Trinidad, or exploring the significant differences between the use of a genre of photographs by young people reported in Chapters 2 and 3 and that by older adults as reported in other chapters. So an important context to this study is not so much the history of photography. It is rather the particular histories of photography in England and Trinidad – whether, for example, there was an established tradition of wedding or holiday or school graduation photography.

There is no direct precedent to social media as a form of photography, although Rose uses the term 'visual economy', taken from Poole,[21] to describe the circulation of images that has typically taken place at the domestic level, for example within families. As Slater and others have noted, these domestic photographs, which were also the best previous examples of mass photography, contain their own continuities.[22] At least one of the major theorists within anthropology, Bourdieu, applied his ideas to the study of domestic photography in France.[23] Long before social media, traditional photography clearly included sub-genres connected to social sharing such as wedding photography and holiday snaps. Yet even these were mainly circulated only among family and very close friends. Photography within social media represents a more generalised sharing and an even greater volume.

The emphasis in this book will not be on the relationship between our findings and these academic debates. Instead we try and balance the generalised interpretations of the genres that seem to emerge from the sheer bulk of these postings through the discussion in Chapter 8, which shows that interpretation is highly variable even among the people we study, not only between academics. But the key difference is that the critical judgement of our informants helps us to understand the social mechanism that keeps the range of photos in check and characteristic of that region. Fear of these criticisms and social denigration is the very reason why postings tend closely to conform to local genres and expectations.

The primary focus in this book is to document the main genres of images that we find in both sites in order to compare them, while reserving analysis of the actual usage of social media in each field site for the nine monographs in the 'Why We Post' series. These other books provide the wider ethnography of people's offline and online lives, and so the interested reader might turn to those volumes for a more detailed account of the uses and consequences of images on Facebook.

This book also represents an example of anthropology of photography.[24] However, its main points of reference are rather different from the primary concerns of prior anthropological work on photography that has been more concerned with topics such as colonialism, history and representation. By contrast, social media photographs are far more involved in areas such as communication and tend to be more transient, which lends them to different conclusions than those directed to traditional analogue photography. Further, the prime concern of this book – that is, direct comparison between different ethnographic settings – is surprisingly rare in earlier anthropological studies, even though the discipline often defines itself as comparative. Even the literature within anthropology that focuses upon the use of visual materials in conducting ethnography, which is one of the aims of this book, has in the past been more focused on methodological issues and the problems of representation.[25] A book that is perhaps a little closer to the way we have undertaken our task was Goffman's study of Gender Advertisements,[26] although we have tried to be less selective and more systematic by including quantitative checks.

This book is an acknowledgement that today social media has become almost synonymous with the practice of contemporary photography, the destination to which virtually all contemporary photography is posted.[27] Figures vary hugely in online sources, but typical estimates examined over the course of 2014 suggested that around 350 million photos were posted every day on Facebook, 55 million on Instagram and 600 million on WhatsApp, while 750 million photographs were shared daily on Snapchat. It seems very likely then that photos shared on social media represent the bulk of photographs taken today. Even more are no doubt taken with social media in mind, but then rejected. Our aim is explicitly to acknowledge this and examine the consequences. The next chapter starts with a discussion of the kinds of photographs that in previous eras would never have been shown to others because their quality is so poor. So while we certainly acknowledge that many of the writers mentioned, such as Sarvis and Frohlich or Van Dijck, give a helpful sense of some of the transitions from analogue to digital photography, these may be taken still further in this latest iteration of mass photography.[28]

We also want clearly to acknowledge that even if our focus is just on images on Facebook, these are not limited to photography. On Facebook, personal photographs blend almost seamlessly with a second major class of visual postings: memes.[29] For memes, there is no comparable literature. While we can draw analogies with previous visual forms, memes do not have a comparable historical precedent in the way that digital photography does. Shifman (2013) has a decent go at defining social media memes and their origins[30] – which again is not a task we would attempt. But almost all our informants will share posts that are usually humorous and most commonly employ short text combined with striking visual images which they themselves would now refer to as memes. If we were to be overly oriented in our study to prior academic writing, the problem is that we would then almost inevitably operate a dualist perception that would treat the meme as a new piece of frippery – partly because it has no associated literature – and we would consider the photograph as an authentic craft, linking us to art history partly because it is saturated with such literature. Instead, we feel as anthropologists that our task is to engage equally with whatever our informants post. Such a standpoint requires us to view these two modes as fairly interchangeable components in the way people express themselves, their values and often their relationships online.[31]

2
The English school pupil

How photography helps people to have fun

Photography revolutionised our relationship to time. The assumed transience of all experience was ended by the possibility of freezing a particular moment and retaining it as a record, instantly, without the time and effort required by a painting. Yet this resulted in a paradox. If the intention was to capture and record our transient experience, the photograph itself was a serious act that most often demanded respect. As a result, people usually stopped whatever they were doing and posed specifically for the photograph. So photography is mostly a vast archive of how people posed for photographs. This has its own history, from a time when it was important to look serious to another when you were inevitably ordered to 'say cheese'. The current demand is for authenticity, avoiding images which look at all formal, but this is equally part of a history of posing.

It is still relatively rare to see photos where people seem to have entirely disregarded the act itself. We might have expected this to have arrived with social media, given the sheer ubiquity of photography today. But an inspection of thousands of Facebook photographs taken of young people in The Glades and posted on Facebook suggests we have reached a sort of compromise. They show people attempting to look more spontaneous, but upon inspection it becomes apparent that this 'spontaneous' look is almost as repetitive and rule-based as the prior era of formal posing. Most people now try to look as if their photo is a spontaneous testament to how they are feeling at that moment, but people demonstrate this in a way that conforms to certain genres of poses.

If there is now a responsibility to look spontaneous, as opposed to looking formal or just smiling, this is an awful lot easier to achieve if we develop standard techniques. That way we don't have to think about this every time a camera phone is pointed at us. The photographs of these schoolchildren suggest two currently dominant ways to look informal and spontaneous. The first of these is simply to stick out one's tongue (Figs 2.1, 2.2 and 2.3).

This is culturally specific, since we found 127 examples of such images from The Glades, but only five from El Mirador (Appendix Figure 1). Equally common is to make a gesture with one's fingers – usually two (Figs 2.4–2.5).

Sticking out one's tongue has become a highly conventional pose. Ironically it is most likely an attempt to distance oneself from formal posing

Gesturing with two fingers is another conventional pose that suggests a 'spontaneous' response to being photographed

Even formal poses can be subverted with the two-finger gesture

Although superficially these might have some similarity to US hip-hop style or 'gangsta' style gestures, there is no evidence that they retain such connotations. They seem instead to have become merely another version of sticking out the tongue to show that they are not looking formal or boring.

Exceptions occur when people are supposed to look formal for some special occasion, which for school pupils usually means the school ball. Yet even here they usually manage to slip in a few images that reproduce this distancing from formality (Fig. 2.6). Formal posing or saying 'cheese' was clearly a response to being photographed and an acknowledgement of such. By contrast, although sticking out tongues and fingers is just as much a response, this is not what such gestures are intended to convey. They are rather supposed to say something about the experience people are having – in essence that they are having a great time which happens to be captured by the photographer.

This opens up another possibility. Could it be that taking these photographs is not just evidence that they are having fun, but an act which *contributes* to them having fun? Has taking photographs shifted from being merely a record of experience to a means of enhancing that experience, of making the moment itself better and more exciting?

The best evidence for this shift in the very purpose of photography is to start with their quality, or often their complete lack of it. Many of the party photos posted on Facebook are – to use the modern colloquialism – 'absolute rubbish'. Below are three such photos taken from those posted by school pupils in The Glades (Figs 2.7, 2.8 and 2.9). These images are just a few that have escaped from the process of editing, but they are the tip of an iceberg. In talking to the pupils themselves,[1] and also observing related events, it becomes clear that the vast number of photos which

When posting on social media is just a way to legitimise the act of taking photos, the real purpose of which was to enhance the sense of fun at that time, quality really doesn't matter

are taken today on smartphones are never likely actually to be posted on social media. In a survey of 2,498 schoolchildren we found that the number of photos they take each week is far greater than the numbers they post on sites such as Instagram and Facebook. From our conversations, it appears that many of these photos are taken at parties or other events where people go largely to enjoy themselves. Such photos may be accompanied by texts which attest to how good the party was and point out to others what a good time they missed by not being there.

While at these parties, taking out one's smartphone for a selfie or another photo is a constant activity. What is important is the reaction to seeing someone do this. The people who notice a camera phone being pointed at them not only make these gestures with face and hands. They also embrace each other, make other gestures, shout 'woo woo', or 'nice one' and generally let their excitement move up a gear. It seems that people point their phones partly to encourage the subjects to get more excited, and thereby to have more fun. As a result the quality of the photograph may have diminished, but the quality of the experience has been enhanced. Which is why it really doesn't matter if some of the images look 'absolutely rubbish' and are too dark or out of focus to show anything. Their purpose has already been served by the act of taking.

As so often with innovations, there is a flipside. While having a photo taken can in itself be fun, the threat that it might actually be posted can curb enjoyment. As one school pupil noted, 'you want to be able to do whatever you like at a party, but can't cos you are worried someone's going to take a photo of it. Got to the point where you want to put a phone in a basket'. In short, the true photograph of experience is potentially the most threatening form of image, since it could become a medium of exposure. This is another reason why people may make sure they respond to the camera by making the appropriate 'fun' gesture, rather than just looking drunk or kissing the wrong person.

For these reasons, the dominant image at a certain age is that which provides evidence of enjoyment. Sticking your tongue out and splaying your fingers are the most common gestures, but there are endless ways in which people can don masks, pull a face, look ugly or turn to the side that will have a similar effect. All of these are quite common in Facebook postings (Figs 2.10, 2.11, 2.12 and 2.13).

Featuring this particular style of pose in one's profile picture seems much more common in The Glades, where there are 72 examples. In El Mirador, by contrast, there are only eight (Appendix Fig. 2).

If we view taking photographs as not just a means for recording experiences, then we can point to an obvious analogy. The presence of alcohol has become the single essential visual evidence that young people are enjoying themselves; like the photograph itself, it possesses

There are many varieties of poses that suggest spontaneity and fun

For teenagers, alcohol is often both the instrument and the evidence for the party being fun

a dual role, being both the instrument and simultaneously the evidence for fun (Figs 2.14, 2.15 and 2.16).

Clearly the teenagers are well aware of the parallel between these two: when they realise that they are going to be photographed they very often reach for alcoholic drinks, which are often gestured towards the camera (Figs 2.17 and 2.18).

Once again this is more common in The Glades, where in our sample of the 20 most recent postings 19 people posted 62 such images (Appendix Figure 4); in El Mirador seven people posted 11 such images. But what the Appendix does not show is how much this corresponds to the teenage age group in particular. For El Mirador, there is only a single post by a school pupil with a drink, while in The Glades there are nine school pupils who posted 40 such images.

Occasionally they will add comments and memes on the theme of alcohol, but this is much more common for adults (Fig. 2.19).

The alcohol and the gestures reinforce each other's messages

2.19

I'm not an alcoholic, alcoholics go to meetings.

I'm a drunk, we go to parties.

Memes about drinking are much less common for this age group than for adults

So far the arguments that have been put forward hopefully provide a convincing answer to the question of why these young people take and pose for photographs. But none of this as yet addresses the question of why they post photographs, nor why they post them on Facebook. Once again, talking with them extensively helps to complement what we can gain from observing their activities. About the most misleading comment one could make about teenage posting is to suggest that it is narcissistic or a form of self-expression. The people who say these things actually seem to have spent no time with teenagers.

In conversation, it becomes clear that these teenagers rarely have sufficient self-confidence at this age to be the sole judge even of whether or not they are having fun. What they require is the constant confirmation of their peers. For this they have to perform some action that will elicit a potential response. Such is the sense of necessity for this peer engagement that teenagers feel they have no choice but to present themselves for inspection. Posting is not about themselves: it is about finding a way to connect to others. Narcissism and self-expression implies an autonomy they simply do not possess.

So to return to those party pictures, it seems that members of this age group find it difficult even to convince themselves that they are having a good time without constant external affirmation that things are good. If, however, the evidence is posted, made public and then affirmed by others, they can finally convince themselves that they did have a good time, that the memorialisation is testimony that this was indeed a memorable occasion and possibly even that they are actually reasonably attractive.

However, the issue of posting such photographs on Facebook has become more complex over the last four years. What started as a peer group platform has changed radically as family and other adults have colonised Facebook. These days all school pupils over the age of 16 (which these are) are well aware of the negative implications of posting compromising photographs on platforms such as Facebook where they may be seen by parents and relatives. So in a sense, some of the previous argument was coming to an end around the time this research was beginning. It seemed that is how Facebook had been employed between around 2007 and 2011, but things were changing fast.

By 2012 and 2013 it is quite likely that the more exciting and risky the moment, the less likely it was to end up on Facebook. Many of those photographs have recently migrated to WhatsApp instead. Indeed, a noticeable change occurred between when we first started following these pupils on Facebook in 2012 and when it came to selecting examples for this book in 2015. Significantly, in between the two periods many of these pupils had finished school; it may well be that there is a general feeling that one should 'clean up' one's profile and remove images where one looks drunk and disorderly before moving on to college and work. Certainly such photos were much less frequent at the time of selection compared to when we first encountered the profiles.

I've heard that 4-6 is nap time x

Snapchat images are also now being posted on Facebook

In contrast to this, we are starting to see a trend towards the reproduction of images taken from Snapchat on to Facebook. This implies that people have screen captured such images, intended by the senders to be merely fleeting, and in effect negated the ethos of Snapchat by placing them in the relatively long-term storage of Facebook. While some Snapchat images are more risqué than typical Facebook images, however, others tend to be quite innocuous, as is the example shown here (Fig. 2.20).

If our evidence was only from The Glades, one would be tempted to argue that as photographs taken with a smartphone have become ubiquitous, they have also become more inconsequential; people would therefore pay less attention to their appearance in these photos. Generally the young people in The Glades don't seem to have arranged their clothes when posing for pictures. This may have already been the case with the decline of more formal posing for photographs, and it also may be a harbinger of adult life. As we shall see in Chapter 4, adults from The Glades seem little concerned with what they wear or how they wear their clothes when it comes to photographs posted on Facebook. The problem with this argument is that it is conspicuously not true of some of our other field sites, such as those in South Italy[2] and Trinidad, as evident from this volume. This supports our view that a comparative perspective is important when considering conclusions from the trajectory of a single case.

The 'social' in social media

No one would be surprised that the Facebook profiles of 16–18-year-olds are replete with pictures from parties. An equally predictable genre which is shared with adults is pictures taken on holiday (Figs 2.21 and 2.22). There is something about this genre for teenagers that has more in common with party photos than the vacation shots posted by adults.

If you try and use these images to find out where the young people went on holiday, in most cases you are likely to draw a blank. In previous genres of holiday photography, the whole point was to show where you had been; it was essential to include the iconic images that stand for that place, for instance its most famous monuments (Fig. 2.23).

Such photos do exist from teenage holiday pictures, most commonly when visiting Paris or the centre of London (Fig. 2.24). Yet by

Photos posted from teenagers' holidays often represent the same genre as home-based party images

2.23

A typical holiday photo posed in front of a landmark, in this instance the Eiffel Tower in Paris

Sometimes, but not often teenagers post images of iconic places they have visited

2.24

far the majority of holiday photos continue the prior theme of showing the subjects with other people having fun. They focus on being in the pool, at the bar, on a pedalo, with a cocktail, enjoying the sun and being friendly with each other, but pay little attention to the background.

This extends even to the use of photographs at English music festivals. When attending such events it is impossible not to be struck by the sheer volume of phones being pointed at the stage. So we might have expected that many such images would appear on Facebook (Figs 2.25 and 2.26). More commonly, however, the photos that appear on Facebook will feature the friends they went to the festival with, enjoying themselves or just comprising the audience (Figs 2.27, 2.28 and 2.29).

2.25

2.26

Photos of performers at festivals are far less commonly posted on Facebook than might be expected from the volume of images that are taken

If anything, music festivals provide another excuse to post pictures showing the subject having fun with friends

In general, it is quite rare for these teenagers to post photographs on Facebook without other people – in contrast to the Instagram photographs posted by this same population, which are analysed in Chapter 3 of *Social Media in an English Village*.[3] So the term 'social media' seems particularly appropriate to young peoples' Facebook use, with regard not only to sharing and viewing but also, especially, to the content. The only place on Facebook where it was reasonably common for an individual to appear alone was in profile pictures, consistent with the way in which teenagers discuss Facebook in interviews. They note that Facebook began as a place for interacting with peers, but as those interactions have migrated to Instagram, WhatsApp and Twitter, Facebook turned into the site for sharing with a wider social universe which stretches beyond their family. They are reaching an age when they have part-time jobs, and their work mates are becoming part of their Facebook network.

In testimony to this concern with showing one's social life, perhaps the most common response to being photographed is not just to make a face but also to put your arm around the person next to you – whether this is your boyfriend, your mother or even someone you barely know. To fail to do so might expose you as an unfriendly person or someone who is stiff or formal. In many cases, it appears as though people were asking for a photo to be taken at that moment as an opportunity to make a gesture of friendship such as pointing at each other. Another way of emphasising friendship is simply to be silly together, and many of the photos already shown are examples of this. Sometimes photos posted by teenagers almost look like a competition to see who can look the silliest.

Some friendships count for more than others. Boys have a greater need to be shown alongside girls, especially good looking girls, than the other way around. Furthermore, boys want to be shown with a variety of different girls rather than one regular girlfriend. In conversation, they readily agree that this is an essential part of male machismo and innuendo for when boys are gossiping with other boys. Typically they don't admit this is true for themselves, but say that it is a valid generalisation about other boys in their class. By contrast, girls are much more likely to appear with other girls, and indeed in a twosome with one other girl. Taking 10 examples of each gender from our sample of school pupils, boys had an average of 26 photos taken with just one girl, while girls had an average of 10 photos taken with just one boy. Indeed there are some females where there are virtually no males present at all in their range of photos, other than family members. Whether this is because they are concerned about their reputation, or simply are not yet comfortable with the challenges of cross-gender relationships, is unclear.

English modesty

This preference for showing social situations rather than the individual represents a general trend towards relative modesty and self-effacement that becomes a core theme of the later chapters of this book, where we discuss adult photography from The Glades. Even among English teenagers, we can see that Facebook reveals a world entirely different from Trinidadian teenagers; it also refutes previous claims in the media that teenagers display excessive self-absorption on social media. For example, there are almost no photographs in the English sample showing young people trying to be in juxtaposition with a celebrity or some kind of important person. These photos are also largely not materialistic, in the rather literal sense that they pay very little attention to anything material. This also means that surprisingly little attention is paid to the subjects' own bodies. Outside of occasions such as school dances or weddings, or the Instagram selfie, there are surprisingly few images in which these teenagers appear to be trying to look sexy. Again, outside of these genres few photos show that they have spent money on fashion, although in conversation it would seem many of them care quite a bit about clothes. Shoes seem to appear mainly because the shot is taken from a long distance, not because they posed deliberately to show off their shoes, in contrast to Trinidad. Males more than females occasionally post photos of objects of desire such as this pair of trainers and a car (Figs 2.30 and 2.31), but these are still rare. There are very few shots that highlight jewellery (Fig. 2.32) nor is there anything comparable to the 'bling' culture we see in Trinidad. Exceptions are the few 'selfie girls' (see below). For everyone else, the focus is largely on an ability to express enjoyment mainly through the face, arms and hands. Clothing is usually

Pictures showing purchases or objects of desire, such as these trainers and car, are quite rare

Showing off 'bling' is uncommon in postings within The Glades

incidental and merely something a person happens to be wearing, in the same way they happen to have necks and shoulders.

For some of these school pupils, personal modesty is also evident in their embarrassment at being photographed. Some of the girls in particular have on their walls a complete lack of photos relating to most of the categories so far described. They never pull faces, and their overall look is one that is pretty and constantly smiling. They never appear with boys or at parties. Possibly they have been warned about future employers' investigations, or by their parents, or they may simply be naturally cautious. Some girls also concentrate more on posting in domestic settings and other contexts more commonly associated with adult posting (Figs 2.33 and 2.34). Occasionally they may show images that comprise the same genre of direct self-effacement that becomes a major element of adult posting (Fig. 2.35).

Despite concerns with modesty it is noticeable that in this study no young people at all, including these girls, opted to make their tagged photos private. So although teenagers may cull tagged pictures,[4] they clearly feel it would be wrong to be seen as someone who has failed to share. The implication may be that at this age tagged photography is

Pictures indicating modesty are more common, though domestic settings such as here are rare

A genre of photos around self-effacement and self-deprecation emerges in teenage years and expands with adulthood

seen more as a gift, an element of collective sharing, appreciated in that someone has acknowledged you – rather than, as it is for some adults, a threat or intrusion. As a result, there may be clear differences in the type of photos that appear as self-posted and tagged. In some cases girls seem to be careful to post only demure and respectable images of their own, but have nevertheless allowed plenty of silly expressions and fun posturing to appear on their tagged images.

Other genres

The discussion so far has been dominated by informal settings such as parties and hanging out with one's friends. However, there are also some formal photographs included in these profiles. The most ubiquitous examples would be the school graduation ball since almost all pupils post a large number of these images. For this event the girls wear formal long dresses in bright colours and the boys wear suits. The photography follows long-held traditions of relatively formal posing, both in individual portrait shots and in those of large groups, usually strung out in a line (Figs 2.36, 2.37, 2.38 and 2.39).

The school graduation party is one of the few occasions for formal posing for teenagers

Similar genres might include family weddings or other family occasions in which again the boys wear suits and the girls evening dresses. Occupying a kind of midway position between the more formal and the informal shots is a common genre consisting of around four or five individuals seated on a crowded sofa, with some perched precariously on its arms (Fig. 2.40).

There are a wide range of other genres present which cannot be covered here, since this book cannot hope or pretend to be comprehensive. For example, quite a common theme is photos of having fun in the snow or at home (Figs 2.41 and 2.42).

The figures in the Appendix give some indication of which genres are more or less common for The Glades compared with those for El Mirador. Perhaps the most striking difference is the general avoidance in The Glades of pictures taken at school or in the context of work. If school pictures appear at all, they are most likely to be ways of marking the fact that one is about to leave school, with appropriate captions such as 'the last maths lesson' (Fig. 2.43). Another photo from this genre shows a typical disruption of formality (Fig. 2.44).

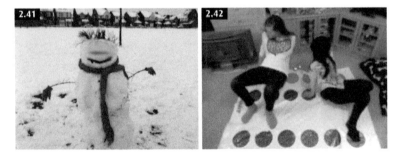

There are a wide variety of genres that signify playing games or having fun outside of parties

A good way to mark the end of schooling is to follow a more formal posed picture with a more disrupted pose

Perhaps the most gendered element of these photographs lies within the genres of sports-related photographs. Males very commonly include such images, which range from going to see football or rugby matches and playing sports to enjoying themselves on winter holidays. Some males post few of their own pictures of any kind, but they seem to have initiated themselves into posting on Facebook (at around 14 years old) by using images of football shirts to mark their team affiliation, such as in early profile pictures (Figs 2.45 and 2.46).

Teenage girls, on the other hand, may post photos of sports (Fig. 2.47), but they do so with much less frequency. A few of them are

Football shirts are a common choice for a teenage boy's first profile pictures

Early postings by teenage girls may include riding a pony, or playing hockey as shown here, but sports are not a major genre

posed with a horse or pony, usually when they were only around 13 or 14 years old, in a this genre that appears to be exclusive to females.

There is very little political comment present on Facebook, other than in the form of jokes. Nor is there much direct comment upon gender relationships of the kind that can develop into often antagonistic banter on Twitter, as described in Chapter 5 of *Social Media in an English Village*. Within more serious postings, gay

Political or issue-based posting is much less common for teenagers than for older adults

rights would be one of the topics more commonly referred to (Fig. 2.48).

The English schoolgirl selfie

One of the key problems with the very word selfie is that it sounds a bit like 'selfish'. The term implies individuals both taking the photo and taking it of themselves.[5] As such, the selfie has become a staple of the media who look for confirmation of their desire to project consumer narcissism on to young people, rather than to conduct any proper appraisal of the phenomenon. The selfish 'selfie' obviously also implies individualism, but this is simply not borne out by our evidence. In the albums we examined there are up to five times[6] as many group selfies taken with other people as there are individual selfies by this age group. This would suggest that, far from being yet another act of teenage narcissistic self-expression (as is generally assumed), the selfie is more a repudiation of the mere self. The single most common purpose of the selfie is to acknowledge a friendship. Quite often it is also the product of time spent with a friend. Sometimes simply taking joint selfies was something to do together for fun. These images are then consistent with what we have argued to be the core role of Facebook: a place where people conduct, display and enact sociality. So it is better to see these as Facebook images rather than 'selfies' (Figs 2.49, 2.50 and 2.51).

The kind of selfie that has been popularised in the media as iconic does exist, but is now more associated with Instagram; if it does appear on Facebook, it is often because it has been re-posted

By far the most common form of selfie posted on Facebook is intended to show friendship rather than individual glamour

from Instagram. This is appropriate since Instagram has become a key site for photography as craft – a genre in which the subject is also something that has been crafted, often food but also clothing and the body, as discussed in Chapter 3 of *Social Media in an English Village*. Out of the 12 male and 17 female school pupils we followed on Instagram, the males had an average of 33 posts each while the females had an average of 147 posts each: that is, around 3,000 images.

Unlike Facebook where, as we have seen, there is relatively little focus on the quality of the photograph, Instagram is much more concerned about photography itself. Even when the same genre appears on both sites, as for example with holiday photography, in the case of Instagram it tends to be just a few selected images that appear – usually chosen because they are the most impressive *images* rather than the most interesting things seen on that holiday. Instagram filters democratise the kind of photographic filters and techniques that were once the preserve only of professional photographers.[7]

Even on Instagram, there is nothing like the proliferation of selfies that has been assumed in the media. Females do post occasional images in which they look particularly good, but at least for this case study there turned out to be only two females who seemed to stand out from the rest in their continual devotion to the posting of individual selfies, thereby matching the popular perception of 'selfie girls' (significantly not a category used by teenagers themselves). A key difference between The Glades and El Mirador is that in the English village such selfie posting seems restricted to the most attractive females who would be seen as appropriate to this category. In El Mirador, by contrast, we shall see that females regard such posting as appropriate irrespective of how 'fit' others may consider them to be.

3
Young people in Trinidad and their continuities

Photos of young people shared on social media are a valuable resource for learning about a society for two contrasting reasons. Photographs provide an opportunity for adults to project their values on to their infants. Once these children grow up, photographs posted on social media then become their first opportunity to establish an autonomous mode of self-expression. In the case of Trinidad, this chapter will show far greater continuity between these two stages, while in The Glades there is a radical break, especially evident when people become parents and mainly signified by the way in which they relate to photographs of their babies. For this reason, the discussion of baby photographs in The Glades appears in Chapter 4 as an aspect of mothering. By contrast, this chapter about El Mirador starts with the posting of babies and continues through to older children.

Families in Trinidad tend to be larger than those in the UK, with an average household size of 3.7 compared to 2.3 in the UK. They are also less dispersed since in El Mirador, unless they migrate, families tend to remain in close proximity to each other, with extended families living in the same area.

There are three main genres of photos posted of babies. The first, also found in The Glades, consists of babies doing 'cute' things, including wearing sunglasses, reading or sitting behind the wheel of a car. In these genres 'cute' implies mimicking activities more associated with adults. The aesthetic suggests spontaneity, often with downward angles that emphasise how small and young the child is. Blurring or poor composition may be retained as evidence of such spontaneity (Figs 3.1, 3.2 and 3.3).

Typical 'cute' images taken by parents

The second genre is of photos that appear to be edited or which form part of a photographic collage. These images typically mark a special event or significant age stage for the child. They may also include effects added through the phone or an editing platform, such as preset borders or embellishments regarded as special or stylish (Figs 3.4 and 3.5).

Photos modified by apps to contain effects or embellishments that are considered special or stylish

This practice of marking special events through the exchange of sentimental notes and gifts contrasts with The Glades, where 'making a fuss' about people has declined and Christmas and birthdays, are now, for most people, the only remaining significant annual celebrations and occasions for gifting. Trinidad, on the other hand, retains a rich tradition of special and social occasions accompanied by card and gift giving, for example graduation, Easter and St Valentine's Day. The sharing of decorative and collaged images online seems to continue the intensive circulation of cards that previously marked such occasions (Figs 3.6 and 3.7). A transitional phase was represented by the mass circulation of e-cards, but today the practice has largely migrated to Facebook where, for example, new parents will circulate photos of their children modified with filters, borders and text.

The continued use of embellishment and decoration within photos provides visual evidence for our larger point about the relative continuity from early childhood into adulthood for Trinidadians as compared to The Glades. In the English case the emphasis is on showing the authenticity of the child as 'natural', which would be diminished by such embellishments, while in Trinidad the continuity comes from an

Decorative or collaged images to mark special occasions

Photo taken by mother to show a spontaneous moment of bonding between father and child

Photograph showing an absent father building a close relationship with his child

emphasis upon how young people are embedded within the family and wider relationships. The profile pictures (Appendix Figure 2) include only 10 instances of embellished pictures in The Glades but 185 in El Mirador, posted by 25 different people.

Mothers in El Mirador post fewer images of themselves holding their babies, partly since they seem to be more often behind the camera. However, this allows them to show more images of babies and fathers where the intention seems to be to suggest a stolen moment of bonding, closeness and relaxation, such as shots of sleeping (Fig. 3.8).

By contrast, fathers make less effort to take and post photos of mothers with their babies. These would indeed look incongruous amidst the bulk of their own postings, which are dominated by topics such as work and sports. The exceptions, noted in the wider ethnography,[1] tend to occur where the father doesn't live with his children (Fig. 3.9). Here photographs are often used to suggest a close relationship between father and child or children, with subjects smiling and often appearing to be on an outing or sharing quality time together.

This reflects a discussion of Trinidadian kinship in our previous book *Webcam*. Here we suggest that, given the frequency with which parenting develops outside of marriage, there is more of an emphasis on the kin role being created directly through appropriate behaviour. That is to say, a father is someone who consistently acts like an appropriate father even if they are not a husband nor even the biological parent.[2] As a result, absent fathers may often use such images to show that they are doting and have an emotional bond with their child. Text such as 'my baby' or 'my angel', 'he love me' or 'the love of my life' often accompanies these images to reinforce the message.

Family photographs in Trinidad include large extended families

Family gatherings for special occasions such as Hindu prayers in the home

In a similar fashion, posted images of babies are used to demonstrate the significance of wider relations to the extended family. There are often several posts within a parent's profile showing the baby with a cousin, aunt or uncle. Again this contrasts with The Glades where we shall see the baby is more directly identified with, and sometimes subsumes, the category of mother.

In El Mirador, photography is also used to demonstrate bonds beyond the extended family (Fig. 3.10). Proximity and juxtaposition can be used to demonstrate affinity also with a street or neighbourhood, typically including several related families. This makes the experience of growing up very different from in The Glades. One of the reasons the previous chapter focuses so much on peers at school is that children in England are far less likely to have a sustained friendship group based on their extended family. Their photos posted on social media mainly feature their school friends. By contrast, in El Mirador, postings are much more likely to be a record of events at which the extended family came together, with, for example, cousins playing together; these images are then shared through social media with the still wider family. Such occasions, held at home, occur throughout the year, for example weddings, birthday parties and Hindu prayers (*pujas*) to which the entire family and friends would be invited, regardless of religion or ethnic background (Fig. 3.11). Another effect of this is that in El Mirador, babies and toddlers are surrounded by relatives of various ages, while children in The Glades spend most of their time with others of the same age.

As we progress to photos of slightly older children in El Mirador, there is a change in emphasis. Ideally parents would wish to continue to post images of children at play that show spontaneity and authenticity, for example (Figs 3.12 and 3.13).

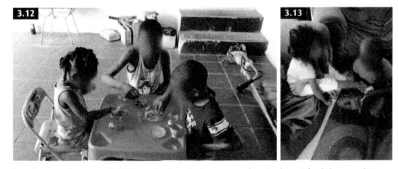

Spontaneous images of children playing. Such young subjects do not feel the need to pose or play towards the camera

As children grow and become conscious of the camera, however, they refuse to acquiesce in the desires of the photographer, insisting instead on playing up to the situation. This becomes the first stage in an important culture of performance and more self-conscious posing for photographs. Children who were previously just playing together now stand as a group and smile when a parent or relative appears with a camera. They also take delight in subverting the intentions of the photographer by taking up postures that their parents regard as 'silly' (Figs 3.14 and 3.15). In other instances they can look embarrassed and awkward, since the choice of that moment to have a picture taken was the adult's and not their own (Fig. 3.16).

Children posing and pulling silly faces for the benefit of the camera

The child in this photograph appears embarrassed; she clearly did not choose to be photographed at that moment

Young cousins pose together for the camera

A common genre at this age is of young children hugging, but with variants. Often cousins or children of family friends are encouraged to 'hug up'. Adults especially like it when the hug is between a boy and girl (Fig. 3.17), since this is seen as especially 'cute'. The children here are cousins, but hugging can be seen as equally natural behaviour for siblings who are posing for the camera.

After about the age of five, children of both sexes start to adopt poses emulating those they have seen adopted by older siblings or relatives. A typical example is young boys who respond to the camera with the 'gangsta' pose (Figs 3.18, 3.19 and 3.20). We also see children emulating the styles of photographs more associated with older people at parties, such as the dancing associated with 'soca' music (Fig. 3.21).

Boys tend to start posing at an earlier age than girls, from around the ages of five to seven. Girls may smile or put one hand on their hip at that age, but they don't seem to experiment with posing as much until they are aged around 10. At around the same age there is also a change in the stance of boys; their pose becomes rather stiffer and more formal – and, one might assume, more self-conscious – compared to when they were much younger (Figs 3.22 and 3.23).

Children mimicking poses they have seen in older relatives, such as 'gangsta' poses for young boys

Children emulating 'wining' as they dance to soca music

Young boys and girls are far less self-conscious in photos compared to when they are older

Trinidadian high school students on Facebook

There is a marked shift in the posting of photographs once children go to school. A prime reason for this is that until then most photographs have been taken by the parents or in the context of home. Such images are either constrained by what the parents want to project or represent the child's attempt to refuse to accede to this. The context for this next stage, by contrast, is photographs in which the child is performing in order to impress his or her peers. Children starting high school are also starting to establish their own social media accounts. This might have brought us closer to the genres found in The Glades – except that, as pointed out in Chapter 2, very few photos posted in The Glades are ever taken at school itself, while this is a common context for peer photos in El Mirador. We shall see below that the same contrast is found with respect to photographs taken at work.

In El Mirador, the bulk of posted photos are taken either at school or in school uniform, mostly by 12–13-year-olds and then again around the age of 17–18, suggesting an emphasis on both starting and finishing high school.

Camera phones and any sort of smartphone are not permitted to be used by students during school hours; if students are caught using a phone at all, it is confiscated. Therefore the majority of images seem to have been taken after school hours, some with children still in uniform and on or near school grounds and others when teenagers visit each other after school or go out to the mall (Figs 3.24 and 3.25).

With young teenagers, we find a marked contrast between single sex and mixed sex photos. Within the mixed groups, the students appear more posed, restrained and self-conscious. By contrast, in single sex images both boys and girls appear more playful and spontaneous (Figs 3.26, 3.27, 3.28 and 3.29).

Teenagers hanging out together during after-school hours

In single-sex groups teenagers seem more relaxed, while in groups of mixed genders they appear more restrained and self-conscious

The one genre that is also found in The Glades is the 'last day of school' photos, where friends sign each others' school uniform and portray themselves loosening up and celebrating. Such images contrast with school outings or photos intended to show achievement, which are common in Trinidad but not in The Glades (Figs 3.30 and 3.31).

In El Mirador both boys and girls also post photos of birthdays at school, including embellished messages and collages of photos that look like a re-mediation[3] of the previous genre of birthday cards (Figs 3.32 and 3.33).

A popular genre of photos posted by boys at school are images showing achievements and sports, especially team sports, that display camaraderie (Figs 3.34, 3.35, 3.36, 3.37, 3.38 and 3.39). Usually these are teams representing the school in competition, but there is particular pride in showing that one is representing the nation of Trinidad (see discussion of nationalism in Chapter 7).

Boys use 'likes' to express interests more than girls, especially to associate with sports and entertainment sites (Figs 3.40 and 3.41). They also post more humorous memes and images around sports, gaming and

Signed uniforms are proudly displayed on the last day of school

Photo collages to celebrate birthdays

interests than they do of themselves (Figs 3.42 and 3.43). This is consistent with a general tendency shared in both field sites for females to define themselves more in relationship to people and males to define themselves more in relationship to things.

Gaming frequently appears in boys' postings, and gaming characters or avatars may be used for profile and cover photos. This seems a genuine reflection of their devotion to gaming because as one student put it, 'yuh come home from school. Yuh can't go anywhere and you don' want to do homework so yuh just be playing games'. We spent a considerable amount of time with young people in internet cafes that were devoted to

Posts by boys indicating friendship gained through team sports and pride in representing Trinidad

after-school gaming. Posts about gaming continue well into adulthood and, in some cases, parenthood. Appendix Figure 4, based on people's last 20 posts, shows 39 posts of gaming by 19 people in El Mirador, but only four images, each from a different person, in The Glades.

If the boys post photos that focus upon sports, games or educational achievement, the girls of El Mirador seem to define themselves more in terms of friendship. Representations of friendship are not restricted to visual posts, but dominate girls' interactions on the public timeline. They include various forms of memes and tags based on

Boys use 'likes' to express interests more than girls do

Boys' posts of interests typically include sports and gaming

a variety of best-friend themes, reminiscent of the BFF ('Best Friends Forever') designation found in The Glades (Figs 3.44, 3.45 and 3.46).

If BFF represents the more benign side to these intense relationships between girls, it can also quickly fragment, leading to various accusations. Social media has encouraged the use of 'indirects', that is, posts about a person or incident which do not explicitly say who or what is being referred to, so that only the people closest to them would

Girls post memes and tags to show friendships and tend to designate BFFs ('Best Friends Forever')

recognise the target in question (Fig. 3.47).[4] Indirects are also expressed through shared memes that contain commentary on ideals around relationships (Fig. 3.48).

Moralising postings which proliferate around relationship issues are also prevalent in adult postings, as seen in Chapter 5. Aspiring to ideal relationships and the desire not to be taken for granted are two themes in #reltalk ('real talk') where, as with the indirect, the sense that a person has been wronged or mistreated is expressed though a generalised moral comment on how people should treat each other

An example of an 'indirect': a post about a person not named in the post

Such a disappointment when you defend someone for so long thinking they are different and they turn out to be just like what everyone said

'Indirects' also include memes that contain moral commentary on the state of relationships

3.49 If u r able to talk shit about me behind my back you are also able to bend over and kiss my ass #reltalk

Like · Comment · Share

3.50 No weapon that is formed against me shall prosper, and every tongue that shall rise against me in judgement thou shall condemn. Isaiah 54 17

Like · Comment · Share

👍 10 people like this

#reltalk, or 'real talk', is another form of indirect. Here a person expresses a general moral comment without naming the person they are referring to

Adults post more explicitly around moralising and relationships

(Fig. 3.49). 'Rel talk' is also often an indirect in which the subject is not acknowledged and only certain people would know the true context.

Adult posting exhibits more explicit moralising around gender and other relationships, and the humour becomes somewhat harsher as compared to that of the teenagers (Fig. 3.50).

An equally important component in the emergence of gender identity is the way in which teenagers start to pose using their own bodies and associated outfits and styles. From quite early on there is a marked and sustained difference between The Glades and El Mirador, with the latter showing more interest in emulating the images of models or celebrities posing in popular media. For women this meant standing with one leg slightly turned out from the body, a hand on the waist or hip, standing to the side with the front shoulder slightly lowered and displaying the behind – either from the side or standing with one's back to the camera, looking over the shoulder. We called these images 'faux model' poses. Appendix Figure 1, based on last 300 images posted, shows 198 such images posted in El Mirador compared to only three in The Glades. Classifying images according to a more general criterion of whether individuals or groups seemed to be drawing attention to what they are wearing, we identified 576 such images in El Mirador and only 142 in The Glades. The latter were almost entirely young people.

Young people in Trinidad, while expending considerable effort on looking good, have little by way of disposable income. So their clothes are mostly very casual, for example jeans and Aeropostale T-shirts (Figs 3.51 and 3.52). Although these come from New York they are not expensive, while still rating as a cut above plain polo or sloppy T-shirts. Teenage girls already have a sense of how to compose a well put-together outfit. If the girl is wearing a pink T-shirt, for instance, she may also have a pink bobble in her hair or pink bracelets to match.

Apart from selfies, teenage girls also post images focusing on parts of the body, such as hair, nails and shoes. Shoes have always been a key component of the wardrobe for women in Trinidad.[5] They are particularly prominent in postings by girls of around 17 or 18 years old, when they start wearing high heels (Figs 3.53 and 3.54).

Teenagers dress casually, but still pay attention to details of coordinating outfits

Teenage girls often display high heels when they start wearing them, usually aged 17 or 18

Teenage girls also reveal experiments with hairstyles

Hair is the principal area of experimentation for girls, based on colours, styles and cuts; it is often piled high and pulled back off the face to show facial features, especially the eyes (Fig. 3.55). We don't yet see weaves or wigs in postings by Afro-Trinidadian teenage girls, but there are lots of plaits, short cuts and different styles (Fig. 3.56). There is also relatively little make-up at this age, with some occasional lipstick but little else. There is also very little of the long hair, hair flicking or hair to the side expressions of femininity that were found among teenage girls in The Glades.

With regard to the wider context of these images there is little of the 'bling' and branded goods associated with adults in Chapter 7, since teenagers do not yet have the requisite income. In fact there are few

3.56

Another example of a photo intended to show off a hairstyle

photos of food, drinks and people eating and drinking together, unless representing an event. In Trinidad, alcohol is more used as an adjunct to showing people enjoying themselves in company, rather than the frisson found among young English people in showing their relationship to alcohol itself. The most common food that appears is Subway or KFC, when kids are hanging out together after school, but the appearance of food in the photo is incidental. Food, drink and restaurants are more prominent when it comes to young adults who are working or are at university.

Having established photo posting norms for young males and females respectively in El Mirador, there are some popular cross-gender genres. An example would be anime, which appears as posts, profile and cover photos (Fig. 3.57). These have emerged from genres associated with younger audiences such as *Pokemon* and *Ben 10*. At that early age the link is more to merchandising. By contrast, the teenagers who would post anime consider themselves to be more creative and artistic, and will often draw and post images of their own art to Facebook.

As in The Glades, it is important to note that Facebook is very much a social media platform rather than merely a place for individual expression. Very few teenagers post regularly on their own timeline. There is the occasional expression of mood, such as comments about how bored they are at school and posts, generally from boys, about sports and gaming. The latter was especially common during the month of the World Cup in 2014, where teenagers commented on matches and declared their

3.57

Anime is another popular genre with teenagers, such as this cover image

Teenagers posted support for football teams during the World Cup

support for teams (Fig. 3.58). However, a key point is that Facebook represents other people's presentation of the person rather than self-expression. Mostly teenagers appear as tagged in other people's shares, memes, events and comments that expect interaction from others, banter or are expressions of their common interests. Most of this sharing and responding is concentrated around the same few people that correspond to their offline friendships and relationships.

It is important to note that simply posting something doesn't necessarily make that action significant. Quite often a person's own postings suggest little concern to curate these images; they are rather a casual dumping of their record from some event, such as a visit to the zoo. In such cases every photo taken is posted into an album which may contain a couple of hundred such photos, no matter how bad or blurry the image (Fig. 3.59). As a result we find some who make a habit of posting everything (600+ photos) and other people who post next to nothing (30 photos); relatively few seem to occupy the in-between position of posting, say, around 100 photos.

Genres of selfies among teenagers

In Trinidad the purpose of selfies seems to be quite different to in the UK and to represent a different aesthetic. As in The Glades, women generally post more selfies than men, although more young men in their late teens and early twenties post selfies, especially if they are more committed to style and fashion. A key difference is that in Trinidad the majority of high school girls post selfies, not simply those considered by others to be the most attractive. Unlike in The Glades, where possessing a certain hourglass shape seems to be the pre-requisite for endless posting of selfies, in El Mirador body type doesn't seem to matter: people taking selfies are of all body types. Teenage girls start to post selfies at around age 12 (Figs 3.60 and 3.61). At that stage they are mainly focused around the face, looking flirtatious or confident, but not overly sexy or provocative. From an adult's perspective, they may suggest the little girl playing an adult. Even girls from stricter or more conservative households will post photos in which they are clearly trying to look their most attractive.

Photo albums are rarely curated and often show all photos taken on an outing, even if several are poor quality

The selfies of older teenage girls don't just concentrate on the face, make-up or the mid-section; they rather tend to present the look or style of a full outfit. Face shots are still common, but equally common are full-length mirror selfies. In some cases the camera phone obscures the face

Teenage girls start posting selfies alone or with friends from age 12

Selfies also appear deliberately to show an outfit

completely, so that only the outfit, or the top half of the outfit, can be seen (Fig. 3.62).

There are other clear contrasts with The Glades which are evident from Appendix Figure 3. Since pretty much anyone in Trinidad is comfortable posting a selfie of themselves alone, far more selfies of this kind are found in El Mirador – 557 compared to 138 in The Glades. In The Glades most young people emphasise selfies that are used to demonstrate friendship with others, rather than the attempt to achieve a certain individual look. So there are 474 selfies with more than one person compared to 116 in El Mirador. The latter also has more mirror selfies, and selfies in which girls are clearly trying to look 'hot'.

Trinidadian teenagers do pull faces in photos, which usually represent them having fun out in public somewhere or with someone (Figs 3.63 and 3.64). What is missing is the use of such actions as an act of self-deprecation, as found in The Glades.

Another genre of selfie that seems completely different from The Glades is the 'sleepy' or 'intimate' selfie. These are usually taken on a bed where the girl is horizontal, sometimes resting on a hand or on a pillow, wearing little to no make-up; she usually stares straight at the camera and is fully clothed or wearing a strappy top (but never pyjamas or overly casual clothes only worn at home). The look is intended to be natural, but in fact the girls look as if they have styled themselves

Teenagers pulling faces in selfies

The 'sleepy' or 'intimate' selfie is taken before sleeping; perhaps taken in the context of a relationship, such photos may be intended to be seen by a boyfriend

to look especially 'natural'; certainly they don't look messy. Around 50 per cent wear headphones and the photo is taken either with a camera phone, where you can see some of the extension of the arm, or a webcam (Figs 3.65 and 3.66). There is an element of an 'indirect' about the 'sleepy' selfie, in that it seems to suggest that the girl is in a relationship with a boy and the photo is mostly taken to be shared by webcam, chat or WhatsApp. This sort of intimate photo suggests that the girl could be lying next to a person, and it is intended for their view. Examples of updates and comments that appear next to this genre of selfie include 'I miss you', 'missing my boy' or 'you're too sweet'. Such intimate selfies seem to compensate for being unable actually to fall asleep with the person indirectly referred to in the post.

Among young people there are also 'boredom' selfies, such as selfies accompanied by the status 'I'm bored', 'so bored' or simply 'boredom selfie' (Fig. 3.67). They appear to be slightly tongue in cheek as well, since some pose with more animation and style than their 'regular' selfies. Some girls also take boredom selfies with one or a couple of other friends.

Few boys post selfies, and when they do, as in The Glades, they need a reason to legitimate this action such as 'I am somewhere important' or 'I am experimenting with art, drawing, animation or something that requires skill'. While young

An example of a 'boredom' selfie, apparently taken simply to pass the time

Selfies posted by boys tend to show them with friends or to be tongue-in-cheek

men want to show that they look good or to show off their outfit, they generally don't want to appear overly vain. As a result far more photos of young men are taken by others rather than as selfies (Figs 3.68, 3.69 and 3.70).

As we shall see in Chapters 5 and 7, selfies are most commonly posted by young women who are post-high school but pre-family. They post selfies that emphasise a lifestyle that includes work, if they have a job, which in turn allows them to wear nice outfits, experiment with their hair, make-up and clothes alongside friends. Middle-class and upwardly mobile women post more selfies on Instagram, using filters, collages and embellishments, than they do on Facebook.

Coming of age and becoming (not just) parents

We noted earlier that teenagers in El Mirador post photos of mixed gender socialising less frequently than socialising segregated by gender. Graduation photos seem to be the rite of passage after which this pattern shifts. For teenagers that go to brother–sister schools, where a boys' school and a girls' school share co-educational activities, students may have friends from the other school, but the majority of their time is spent with peers of the same sex. Graduation is an opportunity to suggest that

Celebrating graduation from school with peers

they are no longer children or students. While they continue themes of achievement and accomplishment, we also see the first unashamed performance of sexuality, through kissing and hugging friends of the opposite sex and especially through the Trinidadian dance style known as 'wining', discussed in detail in Chapter 5. Often they include both more formal 'before' shots and more celebratory partying or 'after' photos (Figs 3.71, 3.72, 3.73 and 3.74).

Graduation is a bridge rather than a break which seems to reflect a much greater emphasis on continuity in El Mirador than in The Glades. The most significant instance of this emerges in Chapter 4 where we shall examine how parenting is seen as a marked break for people in The Glades; as part of this, adults try to 'cleanse' themselves from associations with youth. By contrast the emphasis in El Mirador is on continuity, with mothers continuing to show themselves as attractive based on the cultivation of individual style. Rather than being seen 'only' as mothers, they still dress and pose much in the same way as they did prior to motherhood, emphasising their attractiveness and ability still to look 'hot'. At certain times of the year, for example Carnival and during the pre-Carnival parties locally called 'fetes', parents rarely show themselves with their children at all (Figs 3.75 and 3.76).

At pre-Carnival events parents still emphasise individual style and attractiveness

Individual style, appearance and personality are important to mothers of all ages, as shown in this range of photos

Even for mothers of teenagers or adults, appearing attractive remains important – as does the continued cultivation of individual style and personality (Figs 3.77, 3.78, 3.79, 3.80, 3.81 and 3.82).

Conclusion

This chapter has demonstrated one of the core purposes of this volume: to use cross-cultural comparison as a way to highlight differences between El Mirador and The Glades. With regard to almost every genre of posting we have found marked contrasts between the postings of young people in the two field sites. So, rather than a global common culture of youth, there seems to be just as many differences between these regions in this age group as in any other. We are able to draw on quantitative evidence from our survey of thousands of images, as well as the many selected here to illustrate our qualitative sense of difference. The reason we have gone into such descriptive detail is to try clearly to establish the nature and extent of these differences.

This chapter is also intended to lay the groundwork for establishing themes in Trinidadian posting that become both clearer and more prominent with adulthood. Genres such as selfies and the focus on style and humour will continue to appear across the different age groups. The same is true of themes such as commenting upon gender, moralising and expressing both religious and nationalist sentiments. But while these themes continue, different age groups may express them through different genres. Moralising, for example, takes the form of 'rel talk' and indirects in younger years, but then migrates largely to memes in the postings of adults. Nationalism appears at first mainly in relation to sports, competition and achievement at school. Later on, in adult postings, it is increasingly expressed through vocational activities and overt images such as flags. Other themes discussed here in relation to 'rel talk' and indirects will later manifest themselves more fully as *bacchanal,* the defining character of Trinidadian society.[6]

The reasons why such acute differences between The Glades and El Mirador persist is because postings are expressive of much wider differences in cultural and social norms. We saw that people in El Mirador are enmeshed in a larger set of relationships from childhood, so more photos appeared of babies and toddlers with their extended family than in The Glades. Other differences in kinship structures are also apparent through these images, such as those of absent fathers in Trinidad. For Trinidadians the very concept of family implicates a much wider network than the domestic and nuclear family typical of The Glades. A sense of ancestry and family continuity is also more important, forming one part of a wider set of values for which we use the label 'transcendence' in Chapter 7 and which is most fully expressed through the festival of Christmas.

Over the course of this chapter we have seen how young people start to become socialised into gender roles and social norms. They emulate the poses and behaviours of adults and older siblings, for example the 'gangsta' V-shape fingers for young boys, and starting to pose as 'hot' or feminine for girls. Style and aesthetics around personal image are already shown to be important – not only through dress, consumption and hair, but also through the embellishment of images. In Chapter 5 we will consolidate this examination around structural categories of gender, class and ethnicity, showing how they intersect in complex ways.

A final characteristic of Trinidadian posting that reflects an important general consequence of social media is the emphasis upon the visual – something we shall see later on developed through the usage of memes, but which is prefigured here in textual genres such as the 'indirect'. As the book progresses we shall see how this increasing use of visual communication is important not only for the anthropologist, who is now able directly to 'see' the way in which values are expressed, but also for the population of El Mirador. Here people exploit this new media to associate themselves with what will emerge as the core opposing values of parenthood: domesticity and the values of the family on the one hand and the public world of the street and sexuality, as epitomised by Carnival, on the other.

4
English adults

In Chapter 2 it was suggested that by the ages of 16–18, various social distinctions are already starting to emerge in The Glades. By far the most important appears to be that of gender: for example, we were able to designate a group of 'selfie girls' but not one of 'selfie boys'. Other than that, the most important category seems to be merely being a teenager. This chapter explores social distinctions further, examining the sharp break between being at school and being an adult, observed particularly among women. As an adult there seems to be more concern with what particular 'sub-species' of adult one is becoming. In this short chapter we start with perhaps the most profound example, when a woman becomes a mother, before going on to examine other social distinctions such as class and a further elaboration of gender contrasts.

We saw in the last chapter that in El Mirador there is considerable continuity between the Facebook posting of adolescents and adults. Things are very different in The Glades. At both sites, college and university-age students tend to be less present since they often live away from home, but the focus upon work that becomes of central importance within El Mirador is largely ignored in The Glades. In El Mirador 13 of 19 adult selfies are clearly taken in a work situation, but none in The Glades are taken in the workplace (Appendix Figure 4).

Instead the next major usage of Facebook is a flood of images associated with parenthood, largely motherhood. As other studies have argued,[1] at the time of childbirth two new people are born – the infant and the parent. This life change involves not just new responsibilities, but often an entirely new set of friends and usually the repudiation of a prior lifestyle: mothers typically give up not just on partying but also, for a period, on work. Facebook was designed to be, and initially was, exclusively a young person's platform; the recent embracing of it by adults has been quite rapid. So it was not that the young Facebook users grew up.

It was rather people already in situ as adults who needed to find a way to create their own Facebook – one clearly differentiated from that of youth. Previously they had castigated teenage use of Facebook as a trivial waste of time. How could they then transform it to accommodate their own purposes? One of the key instruments used in The Glades to accomplish this task was the 'no make-up selfie'.

How Facebook grew up

Facebook was not the only platform associated with young people; this has also been true of both Instagram and Snapchat. Rather different was Twitter, which was seen as appropriate for adult use, especially in relation to obtaining information. Indeed adults in The Glades seem entirely unaware of the very different use of Twitter for the kind of peer banter they associate with Facebook, unless they have school-age children.

Apart from Twitter the denigration of social media has become something of a national pastime. Criticism is sometimes aimed at Facebook, but at other times it is aimed at the general devotion of young people to screens; more recently it re-surfaced as a critique of the selfie. These criticisms were seen as evidence of the way social media has emphasised the most self-absorbed, superficial and narcissistic aspects of youth. Adults in general blithely ignore the evidence given in Chapter 2 that all three practices are in essence social, not individualistic. The problem for adults who now wanted to colonise Facebook is that they first needed to cleanse Facebook of these earlier connotations in order to make it a more respectable site for their own postings.

Ironically it was a selfie that proved the most effective means for this task of purification – more specifically the 'no make-up selfie'. Looking across the profiles of the adult women in The Glades whom we followed, it was striking that many posted a 'no make-up selfie', even though most of them had never previously posted a selfie of any kind. When the 'no make-up selfie' appeared in March 2013 most of the journalistic attention focused on three components. The first was its sheer level of success, raising 8 million pounds for UK cancer charities in around a week; the second was the participation of various celebrities and the third was a critique of this phenomenon. One of the clearest examples of the last was by journalist Jenni Murray.[2] She pointed out that while no one can begrudge the successful fund raising, people suffering from cancer have grounds for viewing this as a kind of unfortunate pastiche/parody of the deterioration in their appearance that occurs with cancer, and especially with chemotherapy. As Danny, the ethnographer, was spending a day per week working with hospice patients at this time, he could attest to these patients' desperate need to retain their dignity during cancer. The grounds for this critique are thus very clear.

This was not, however, the intention of those who participated in this genre, who would most probably have been horrified to think that they had given offence. Our evidence was that the success of this campaign was only tangentially about cancer; the true purpose was directed at the more immediate concerns of those who took part. This campaign proved an excuse to do two contradictory things at the same time. One is that when a phenomenon becomes as huge as the selfie, and is also associated with the young, large numbers of people want to take part and to post at least one selfie. At the same time, adults in The Glades rather enjoy denigrating the young and were reluctant to let go of their critique of selfie culture.

The 'no make-up selfie' provided a means both to post a selfie and at the same time actively to express a critique of prior selfie culture. It was distanced from individual vanity by being a social process, based on being nominated by others. It repudiated the aesthetics of the idealised selfie by showing people at their least glamorous. Unlike some celebrities, most of the people in The Glades didn't just decline to wear make-up. They clearly aimed for a kind of truth-telling 'warts and all' look. In short they used it to critique not just the selfie, but also the much wider social pressure to appear glamorous and made-up for social consumption. Three women noted that they don't actually wear make-up anyway, and so this was their normal face (Figs 4.1, 4.2 and 4.3,)

Some went a stage further in trying to use this device to create something entirely opposed to the dominant image of the selfie. For instance one woman clearly felt that since she also never wears make-up, a 'no make-up selfie' seemed a bit of a cheat. Her solution to the problem was to post a picture of herself side on. Because, as she says in the accompanying comment, this is the perspective that she really doesn't like and generally feels quite self-conscious about (Fig. 4.4).

By creating a serious and unglamorous version these women felt able to appropriate the selfie for themselves, and to link it to what we will see are their own core projects of modesty and authenticity. The situation is very different in El Mirador. Here the selfie becomes a means for showing continuity between young people and adults, since no one is seen as 'too old' to pose for a glamorous selfie.

Although posing for 'no makeup selfies', it was important for these women to note that they don't usually wear make-up anyway

One woman showed what she considered to be her least attractive side

The infant

Anyone who has had a baby recently in England, or who knows someone who has, will be aware that many new parents seem continually engaged upon an anxious quest to determine whether their new infant is doing the same thing as all the other infants born at the same time, or ideally a little bit sooner. The development of ante-natal classes and toddler groups has created a new type of age-bonded peer group. Historically babies used to be contrasted more with other family members of disparate ages, but now they are related to a specific cohort all born around the same time, which is likely to have contributed to this anxiety and

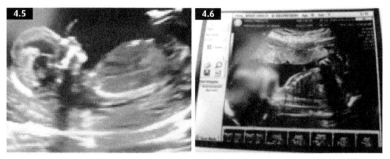

As yet there is no consensus as to whether it is appropriate to post ultrasound foetal images on Facebook

desire for comparison. For many new mothers Facebook is becoming an increasingly integral part of this process.

For most mothers having a baby in The Glades meant first a period of time out of work and second a clear and explicit need to make new friends and to create a support network, thus easing the transition into becoming a parent. Incessant posting about one's new baby by new mothers has become a cliché; it is something everyone is now self-conscious, and frequently apologetic, about. Some decide not to post at all, but most do post frequently. This usually receives considerable numbers of positive responses from two audiences: existing family and the new set of friends that has developed around these ante-natal classes and post-natal toddler groups. The wider ethnography showed that this is the single most important period for making lifelong friendships.

As yet there is no clear consensus around the appropriateness of posting images taken from ultrasound, although in some countries, especially in South America,[3] this is already an established genre. Based on the rather small sample of this field site, this practice seemed more common among lower-income families, but instances among higher-income families also occurred (Figs 4.5 and 4.6).

The ultrasound is a very direct way of letting people know that one is pregnant. But, as so often in The Glades, it is more common for messages to be delivered on Facebook in some form of indirect mode that could be considered amusing. One strategy was simply to show baby clothes, which also meant a declaration of the gender of the forthcoming infant, often with some kind of associated message. In this case it was 'My first "it's a boy". If anyone wants to get rid of any baby boy stuff let me know' (Fig. 4.7).

Displaying clothing is one way of hinting at the gender of the forthcoming baby

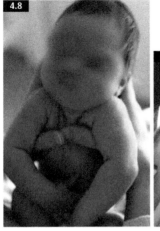

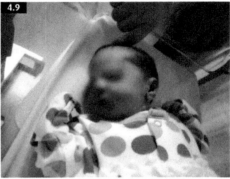

Very first images of newborn babies

As pregnancy develops some mothers may also post photos of their 'bump', though again there is no consensus on how appropriate this is. In the 1960s there seemed to be developing a genre around filming and recording births, but not only is this absent from Facebook, today it seemed as if all traces of the birthing process should be removed prior to posting.

Once the infant is delivered, however, we can start to identify certain clear genres of posting as being common or typical. These in turn suggest emerging standards for how infants should be visually presented to the social media public. For example, it seems almost obligatory to post pictures of the newborn baby very soon after birth. Often the baby is shown asleep or cradled in hands and arms. Most are clothed or in a nappy, but some remain naked (Figs 4.8 and 4.9).

The next most common genre seems to be a photograph of the baby either smiling or with an expression that could be interpreted as a smile (Figs 4.10 and 4.11).

As the babies become toddlers the range of photographs expand, but certain shots again seems characteristic and common. Three of these are illustrated here. The first is the photograph of the infant wearing sunglasses. For reasons that are not clear (no pun intended), this is a very common genre in The Glades (Figs 4.12, 4.13 and 4.14).

The second set of images that seem to correspond to a distinct genre are those of the infant whose face is smeared with food, revealing him or her to be a 'messy eater.' For the messy eater shot, chocolate usually plays an obliging role. Typical captions to such images would be

The first smile or something approximating to a smile is a very common genre for posting

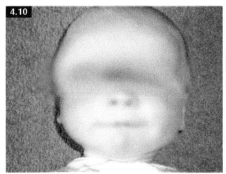

We are not sure why toddlers in sunglasses have become quite such a popular subject for posting

'loved it mum', 'When friends mind your baby ...' or 'The joy of chocolate cake!' (Figs 4.15, 4.16 and 4.17).

A generation earlier, the equivalent photo might well have been exactly the opposite: a scrubbed baby in a clean bib. The transformation

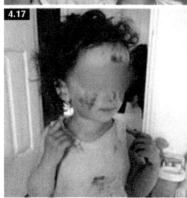

The messy eater is a favourite genre accompanied by some suitable comment

is characteristic of a more general shift from formal posing to informal expressions of authenticity as discussed in Chapter2.

Other genres include an infant posed behind some kind of wheel, ranging from a toy to being placed in the driver's seat of a real car (Figs 4.18, 4.19 and 4.20).

Typical captions might be 'got a bit more nervous when C...took to the controls!'

It is perhaps surprising how much the individual baby shots dominate over those featuring family and parents. There are some more formal shots of the baby with proud parents, as well as usually some images of mothers looking adoringly at their infants, or just looking happy (Figs 4.21 and 4.22).

However, these are much less common than pictures of the infant alone. Such images are twice as common in The Glades as in El Mirador, seeming to echo our ethnographic sense of the stronger emphasis upon kinship and relationships in the latter site. If there is an older child in The Glades, however, parents may try and arrange them in a reassuringly caring pose in relation to the new infant (Fig. 4.23).

Infants are often photographed posed behind a wheel, belonging to either a toy or an actual vehicle

Mothers will often post images of themselves in the act of adoring their infants

In this reassuring image, the older child is placed in a caring position in relation to the baby

The situation is more complex than just whether kinship itself matters because there is also the question of what form this kinship takes. Again the images reflect our ethnographic findings. For Trinidad the focus is on the extended family, as will be discussed in the next chapter, while people in The Glades almost always focus on the nuclear family as the kin context for the child. Specific representations of the child in a nuclear family are therefore more common in The Glades, where 29 people contribute 136 posts that are probably showing such nuclear family relationships (it was not always clear if this was the case). In El Mirador, by contrast, we find 15 people posting 27 examples (Appendix Figure 4). Also in The Glades it is much more common to include some form of more professional family photographs, or the family represented within a collage. These may simply reflect a conservative retention of the family portrait, once an important and popular genre of photography (Figs 4.24, 4.25 and 4.26).

Moving to the event

Posting babies and infants does not seem to require any justification other than the desire constantly to re-acknowledge their presence. As the toddler becomes a child, however, the convention shifts to something closer to the dominant form of adult posting. In this one posts largely to acknowledge some specific event or moment that warrants this public exposure, rather than merely posting on a whim. Most shots of older children are therefore accompanied by texts that explain the 'point' of the posting. In the case of children, the photo often documents the first time something happens, for example: 'First night in her new butterfly princess room for a "big girl"'; 'first potty'; 'first day at school' (Figs 4.27, 4.28 and 4.29). Other examples include playing football, acting in a school play or formally dressed for a wedding – as well as occasionally for other events such as Halloween

4.24

A professional photograph or similar image is often used to idealise the family as a whole

Posting pictures of older children needs the wider legitimacy of an event, for example the first day at school or the first night in a new room

Other subjects worthy of posting may include a school play, a sports competition or dressing-up games

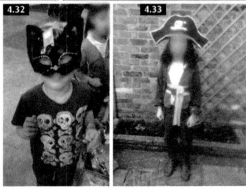

(Figs 4.30, 4.31, 4.32 and 4.33). The point at which infants are portrayed in clearly gendered roles differs among parents, though girls are usually feminised from quite early on.

Another common genre is of photos that depict a child's birthday, frequently posted in both sites (Figs 4.34, 4.35 and 4.36). In El Mirador we find 10 people posting 18 examples of birthday pictures, while in The Glades we have 18 people posting 29 examples (Appendix Figure 4).

Adult posting

No excuse is needed to post an image of an infant. For adults, however, merely posting one's mood or trivia may be seen as relatively immature; it is a practice they often condemn. The two main justifications for adult posting are either humour or as the commemoration of an event. Some continuity with childhood posting exists, for example an event such as a birthday, with adults increasingly sent the kinds of birthday acknowledgements established some years ago between children. Adults tend to post more texts and fewer photos than children and adolescents, though they may also post humorous images such as cartoons (Fig. 4.37).

Older children are treated more like adults, with the birthday becoming the most common reason for posting on Facebook

In terms of annual events the one that clearly stands out is Christmas, a reflection of a more general trend in which the single festival has gained prominence at the expense of other annual or religious festivals.[4] Christmas is most commonly represented on Facebook through its most visual icon, the Christmas tree (Figs 4.38, 4.39 and 4.40).

Sometimes more indirect ways are used to reference such celebrations. In these images food has been used, illustrating both a traditional Christmas dinner and a classic Shrove Tuesday ('Pancake Day') meal (Figs 4.41 and 4.42).

Older adults may prefer to post under the guise of a cartoon rather than a photograph

In the same way that Christmas dominated annual celebrations, weddings clearly dominate over all other life cycle events. This also reflects the huge importance of wedding photography as an established tradition (Figs 4.43, 4.44, 4.45 and 4.46).

Outside of birthdays, weddings and the associated stag/hen parties (see below), posting life events is not very common. Yet Facebook has become increasingly important in relation to death and its public

Almost the only annual event that necessitates Facebook posting, other than birthdays, is Christmas

Festival foods such as a Christmas dinner or Shrove Tuesday pancakes are also posted

acknowledgement. For example, one of the older males who passed away towards the end of this research period received a total of 75 messages acknowledging this event and expressing appreciation of the man. But this topic is not covered here since such posts tend to be textual rather than visual. Images are more common in postings around the anniversary of deaths, mostly of parents. The deceased may be represented as elderly, but photographs of them when young are quite often used. Memes are also possible features of such memorials (Fig. 4.47).

There are two major continuities with pre-social media photography genres, one of which is the wedding photo

Perhaps the single most common reason why families took photographs over the last few decades has been to record holidays.[5] Classic holiday pictures might be taken at the seaside (Figs 4.48, 4.49 and 4.50). This genre remains hugely important for adult posting. Furthermore, the older the person is, the more likely that his or her Facebook postings will be largely dominated by albums of holiday photos, representing pretty much a direct migration from physical albums to social media.

One popular variant is showing oneself in winter clothing, even in summer (Fig. 4.51), while other typical holiday photos within England depict funfairs, castles, iconic London settings, the zoo and sunsets (Figs 4.52, 4.53, 4.54 and 4.55).

I Wish R.I.P Meant
"Return If Possible"

Facebook has become a key site for memorialisation of the dead

The other example of continuity in genres is the holiday snapshot

Unpredictable English weather is often the focus of ironic beach photos

Typical holiday snaps show a range of situations and photogenic moments from the trip.

Visiting gardens is a popular pastime in the English site

Photos of holidays abroad typically show people enjoying out of the ordinary activities

Photographs taken while visiting gardens are also common (Figs 4.56 and 4.57).

Holidays taken abroad are more likely to include skiing and sun-bathing, iconic monuments and cruising (Figs 4.58, 4.59 and 4.60).

Holiday photos constitute a major genre within The Glades, with 1,199 such postings as compared to 243 in El Mirador (Appendix Figure 1). This may be partly because people in The Glades are more affluent and so have more holidays. But it also seems consistent with the general point that English posting may be more conservative in retaining prior genres of photography.

It was noted in Chapter 2 that the distinction between youth and adulthood is so important that it tends to mask other forms of differentiation, with the exception of gender. However, adulthood is the time when people are more readily identified around a variety of distinctions. Gender remains the most important, but class, sexual orientation and politics may also become significant. For anthropologists each of these tends to be seen in relational terms. As such, the visual representation of adulthood is a good place to explore the way some of these categories are constructed as systematic oppositions.[6]

Masculinity

The selection is not intended to represent all men in The Glades. Elderly men, for example, would be less useful in characterising any overt masculinity. Instead, these images represent what could be considered the 'core' of Leeglade – that is, men in their twenties to forties working in the service industries or self-employed. These are the people whom one is most likely to meet at pubs and who retain genres of male socialising offline as well as online. For such men there seems to be more continuity between teenage posting than for females, which accords with stereotypes in England that characterise young men as 'immature' relative to young women. Some of these are simply continuities of genre, for example postings from music festivals, although we can see more focus on the event and performances and less on one's companions than in young people's postings (Figs 4.61, 4.62 and 4.63).

Men often post their festival photos with an emphasis on crowds and spectacles

The unpredictable English weather is a common subject for posting, as it is of everyday conversation

The population here being English, there are also frequent references to the weather (Figs 4.64 and 4.65).

There is limited continuity with some of the conventions of teenage poses. So occasionally we see tongues sticking out and other gestures, though these largely fade away as men get older (Figs 4.66, 4.67 and 4.68).

There are far fewer party pictures trying to demonstrate that the subjects have had a good time. The one such genre that seems to increase in importance is that based around wearing fancy dress (Figs 4.69, 4.70 and 4.71). Such postings are a good deal more common in The Glades than in El Mirador (Appendix Figure 1), with 178 examples compared to only 31.

The strongest elements of continuity for male postings are images related to football and drinking. Several of the 20- to 30-year-old males in The Glades play football, and practically all actively follow the Premier League and a local club. Major matches appear either as spectacles or images that testify to attendance (Figs 4.72 and 4.73).

Occasionally we see 'teenage' genres retained, for example sticking out tongues, but these decline with age

A very popular genre in The Glades is posting people in fancy dress

Photos depicting attendance at football matches are a common theme for men

Photos of individuals playing football are also common

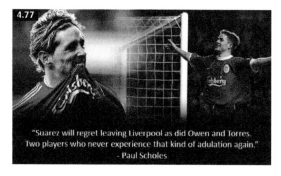

Memes about football remain common for older males

"Suarez will regret leaving Liverpool as did Owen and Torres. Two players who never experience that kind of adulation again."
- Paul Scholes

There may also be shots of the men playing football (Figs 4.74, 4.75 and 4.76) and, as with teenagers, there will also be memes or comments about football (Fig. 4.77).

As with all the themes for male posting, if a post can be given a quirky or funny edge, or associated with toilets, then it probably will be – as in this picture of a urinal (Fig. 4.78).

A new genre of posts among men in The Glades are images showing how males manage to watch football notwithstanding the pressures to adapt to domestic life as parents and householders. This might include a posting explaining how one has installed 3D television in the living room, or how one has set things up so as to continue watching while doing the washing up (Figs 4.79 and 4.80).

This intense male orientation to football is the main reason why people in The Glades post 251 photographs of sports compared to 65 for El Mirador (Appendix Figure 1). The figures are closer in terms of sports images considered important enough to post on their walls shown

Men also like to post humorous images, such as this picture of a urinal

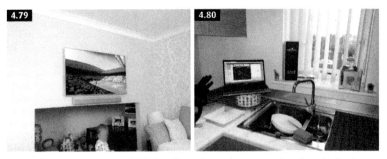

Males will post ingenious methods they have devised to ensure that they don't miss sporting action while occupied by domestic tasks

in Appendix Figure 4. However, the El Mirador images focused upon the World Cup, while those from The Glades tended to be broader and to include the personal involvement of the person posting.

Adults are generally less worried about being seen in association with alcohol on Facebook than teenagers who might be viewed as underage. At the same time there is less of a frisson of drink as an instrument in showing how good a time one is having than in teenagers' postings. Instead it is simply the expected accompaniment to life. So compared to the postings of teenagers in The Glades, adult postings are more likely to be simply photographs of drinks or of men drinking mostly beer (Figs 4.81, 4.82, 4.83 and 4.84). Men seem happy to replicate these genres whether at home or abroad. For example, one of these is a holiday shot from Bulgaria, but it could equally well have been taken in England.

Young adults often include sporting activities among their holiday shots, though this may be found for both females and males (Figs 4.85 and 4.86).

Occasionally postings relate to more explicitly 'laddish' behaviour such as vomiting in a toilet, peeing in public, getting a black eye, falling asleep drunk in a street, taking a photo of a mate while they were sleeping or anything else that gives the connotation of having had a 'rough' – that is, a good – night out (Figs 4.87, 4.88, 4.89, 4.90 and 4.91).

What are missing in The Glades, which only becomes apparent when we compare these images to El Mirador, are photographs that simply focus upon a male trying to look good. This represents a major difference between the two field sites. Indeed males in The Glades are generally less inclined to post images of themselves alone, with 359 examples compared to the 696 examples of Trinidadian men (Appendix Figure 1). What the two sites have in common is that men are far more concerned

Beer is established as the expected accoutrement to adult male life

Young males often include sporty activities in their holiday postings

to show themselves in direct association with an individual female than females would be to associate themselves with an individual male. In The Glades the average male has 16 photos of himself with one other woman, while the average female has only seven images of herself with one other male (Appendix Figure 1). Men may not care about the clothes

Laddish behaviour on holiday signifies having had a good time

they wear, but they certainly care about which women they are associated with when being photographed.

Rather than posting images of themselves, men will often present themselves vicariously though association with objects. We have already seen this with football and drink. Another instructive genre was food. At least among the football-oriented group, food was not shown as examples of craft or skill, but rather directly to proclaim 'masculinity'. Types of food posted included burgers, chips, crisps, steak sandwich, an Indian tikka masala and pretty much anything that is generally considered unhealthy (Figs 4.92, 4.93 and 4.94).

Men in The Glades generally do not post in ways that suggest much by way of aspiration or materialism. This represents a quite remarkable

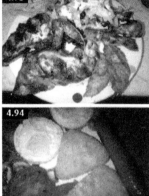

The only food worth posting for many males is that which is conspicuously unhealthy

contrast to most of our other field sites.[7] Just occasionally they will celebrate a purchase or post some item they would like to buy, but this is relatively rare (Figs 4.95 and 4.96).

Perhaps surprisingly, there were no images in this group connected to buying expensive gadgets such as a new phone. Nor were there many postings of cars and motorbikes, with one exception. A much older male had adopted this as his particular grounding for confirming his masculinity, through captions that he himself claimed were clearly intended

It is relatively rare for anyone to post objects that celebrate a new purchase

'Babe' shots are found, but are not common

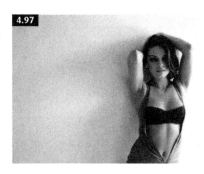

4.97

4.98

In strong contrast to El Mirador it is extremely rare for people in The Glades to post non-humorous references to sex

to deter any female interest: 'my 1st v8 p6 rover still miss the loopy old bus with its leaky rear axle which meant not much in the way of rear brakes slightly erratic borg warner 35 gear box and rotten rear inner arches so the interior smelt a bit compost heapy but with the twin weber 40dcoe kit it used to eat xj jags and 3 litre capris 4 breakfast.'

An equally strong contrast with El Mirador is that while sex is more common in male postings in the Trinidad site, it has only a very limited presence in The Glades. There are a few 'babe' shots (Fig. 4.97), but any direct reference to sex is extremely rare. Indeed the hashtag that went with this posting may summarise the prevailing attitude:

'so I get into to work to find a present on my desk #awkward' (Fig. 4.98).

The adult female

There is a reason that the last section was given the title 'Masculinity' while this one is called 'The adult female', and also why it will be considerably shorter than the discussion of masculinity. This is because gender is not symmetrical, with women playing a different cultural role than men. In Chapter 6 the topic is 'the Englishness of posting', and the material presented there will be female-dominated. This is because women in The Glades (as in many societies) have a greater responsibility to 'stand for' and objectify wider social values, including English traits such as domesticity and the typical conservative values associated with suburbia.[8] This leaves men freer to use their postings to develop a more specific genre of masculinity. In addition this section is less concerned with older females, the core material being drawn from profiles of mothers in their twenties and thirties. In The Glades we find much less emphasis on anything that might be called femininity. Instead women appear more in terms of social roles and responsibilities, such as mothers and housewives. In Chapter 6 we will look in more detail at this subsumption of the female to their own children and other ways in which women demonstrate modesty and self-effacement. It is discussed there because it also provides such a striking contrast with the postings in El Mirador.

Nevertheless that leaves several contrasts that can be explored here. One of the clearest is that of food and its consequences, an issue of obvious concern to women. It was noted that young men seemed to post pretty much any food that was significantly fattening, presumably as an act of bravado. Women, however, instead of posting images of healthy food, tend to post direct references to their concerns with body size and images as in 'Finally joined the Gym . . . First session nice and early morning.. size 6/8 . . . here I come baby . . . Let the new ME begin . . . !!' The relevant visual postings are dominated by those that make fun of their own constant obsessions with dieting (Fig. 4.99 and 4.100).

Where women post food photographs, these are almost all of food that they have made themselves. Perhaps because the period of this study coincided with the immensely popular television programme

References to dieting, or to being fat, are a very common theme of postings, but only for women

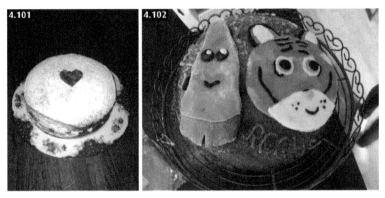

Images of baking were dominated by home baking for the family

The most common object of home baking is the cupcake

'The Great British Bake Off', it was baking that dominated. In addition, because most of the people being discussed here were mothers, the baking was dominated by things made for children and family (Figs 4.101 and 4.102). Within this genre, photos of cupcakes were clearly dominant (Figs 4.103 and 4.104).

Some images also featured cakes made for charitable purposes, alongside homemade jam (Figs 4.105 and 4.106). Other meals that came

It is common to post images of baking, jam-making or other home cooking done for charitable purposes

Good quality cooking or meals were seen as more suited to Instagram than Facebook

Similarly, it is rare to post food made by others on Facebook, though as here a birthday spread is appropriate

out especially well may merit a posting of Facebook, but generally this was seen as better suited to Instagram as a 'craft' picture (Fig. 4.107). It was rare to post food made by others. One example was this spread of pub food that represented a birthday party (Fig. 4.108).

There were no sporting images posted by women that compared in volume and intensity with male postings about football, though several had images from the 2012 London Olympic Games (Fig. 4.109).

Women have no equivalent to football for males, but may occasionally post sports such as the Olympic Games

If men's relationship to alcohol is dominated by postings of beer, as noted above, women have a clear equivalent in wine. The posts generally showed no attempt to claim expertise and connoisseurship of wine varieties, but are rather about a generic category called 'wine'. While men tend to focus on the beer in and of itself, wine for women is in effect a relationship, and mostly a difficult and ambiguous one (Figs 4.110, 4.111, 4.112 and 4.113).

Sometimes, however, certain fickle women will betray this core relationship for another (Fig. 4.114).

The one 'breakout' genre that seems to have developed for young women are hen parties, more common as postings on Facebook than the male stag party. These also allow those who are somewhat older to

One of the most popular themes for female posting is wine as a generic category

revert back to teenage genres discussed in Chapter 2 where people can just look silly (Figs 4.115 and 4.116).

Women will also sometimes post a photo from the various versions of a girls' night out; these are now common and may take place at any time and in a wide variety of venues (Fig. 4.117).

Men rarely post about relationships per se, but relationships in and of themselves are frequently commented upon in women's profiles. Within these there are three fairly equal varieties. The first is posting about one's relationship to men in general (Fig. 4.118).

A 'breakout' genre for female posting has become hen parties

Women also occasionally focus on their relationship to other forms of alcohol

Women post about their relationship to men in general

Women will also sometimes post versions of a 'girls' night out'

The second is posting about one's relationship to children, either as expressions of affection or as the prosaic reality of chores (Fig. 4.119).

Women post frequently about their relationship to children

The third common relationship genre for women is female friendship

The third is a genre of posting about one's relationship to other women as close friends (Fig. 4.120).

The other key area of posting is one of general humour in relation to housework and breaking free of household chores. These are discussed within a more general focus upon humour in Chapter 6.

Homosexuality

We have included a short section on homosexuality for two reasons. First it does something to balance the inevitably crude generalisations around gender that arise when the topic is presented so briefly. The other reason is that it represents a stark contrast with Trinidad, where it is still extremely rare that a person would come out as gay on Facebook. Even in The Glades only two of the people we followed online were explicit about being gay within their Facebook profile, and they represent polar opposites in how this is portrayed. A young lesbian woman has almost no explicit references to this aspect of her life. It is not that she hides it. Simply that you would have to extrapolate this information from the scenes of holidays with another woman and very occasional references in support of gay marriage and so forth. This makes her quite similar to most heterosexuals in this study, who also are generally reticent about matters of sexuality once they are beyond a certain age.

By contrast, a middle-aged male has constant discussions in his status updates in which he vociferously argues about gay rights and other issues. Yet perhaps most explicit are his profile pictures

Some people who are gay almost never mention their sexuality on Facebook, while others make frequent references to it

Memes are often used to oppose anti-gay stereotypes

(Figs 4.121 and 4.122). Other genres include support for gay rights movements, as well as memes that he views as refuting stereotypes of masculinity, almost invariably through humour (Figs 4.123 and 4.124).

Social class

The other contrast that we will briefly explore within The Glades is class. The ethnography of The Glades suggested a rather different conclusion about class from the way it is generally understood in the UK, as a distinction between relatively equal fractions of working class and middle class people. One of the most clear-cut pieces of evidence for something quite different came from these visual posts on social media. In surveys the majority of English people continue to describe themselves as working class, but the same surveys show that the salience of class has declined. As a result class affiliation is not a strong indicator for predicting attitudes to other issues.[9]

Within The Glades it was hard to see any clear distinctions that would correspond to this self-designation. Most people in The Glades seem to post images which would be quite difficult to see as class-specific. The conventional boundary between middle and working class is pretty much invisible, and would certainly not have emerged from the pattern of images posted. For example, every generalisation made in the previous section on gender would have been equally true for people who call themselves middle and working class. Indeed, one could go further and say that we see no evidence from the contents of our study that a class divide is any way apparent from what people post on Facebook.

Instead, there is a single, very clear contrast that pits around 90 per cent of the population in opposition to a specific fraction. The latter represents people who almost all live either within social housing or, in some cases, the cheapest private rental accommodation. Even within that group, however, which represents around 17 per cent of the population, there were those who rejected any association with that context and used education or other means to distance themselves from it. In short, their postings would be much like the rest of The Glades.

What remains then is a group that constitutes probably only around 10 per cent of the population of The Glades or less, though it would certainly be higher in more urban locations. This represents only a small section of those people who would call themselves working class, but this 10 per cent does have a clearly defined accent, language, demeanour and concerns that divide them from the rest of the population. This was clear during the ethnography generally, but becomes especially apparent when we examine their Facebook postings.

They provide an even stronger sense of overt masculinity than the rest of the population, but in their case women would also make a more strident claim to femininity – though this is a femininity that focuses more on being strong than being pretty. Partly this reflects the fact that the group we worked with included several who had become mothers at around 17.

Of the people we came to know well, masculinity was clearly associated with the military and associations with the army. This young

The army is an important route out of low-income areas

People living in social housing are more likely to post images affirming masculinity

male creates his look through a montage of four photo images, including wearing a helmet and being substituted by a tiger (Fig. 4.125).

Meanwhile his friend, who actually is in the army, poses both formally in uniform and armed (Fig. 4.126).

More distinct still were some of the women. They are much more likely to post shots intended to show off sexy clothing or the sense of a strong female character that is more analogous with the machismo of the males (Figs 4.127 and 4.128).

Women in social housing often post as strong characters, complementing those of masculinity

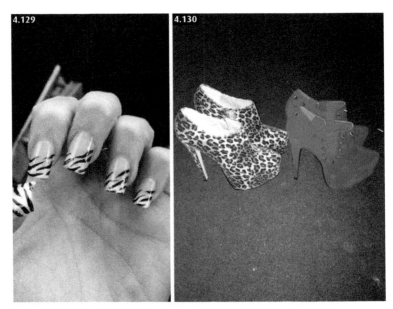

The same women are more likely to refer overtly to a sexy or strong look

Similar sentiments can be expressed through shopping and objects such as these photos (Figs 4.129 and 4.130), with captions that refer to sexy new shoes or nails.

These same women are far more likely to be explicit both with regard to sex and to their own problems (Figs 4.131, 4.132 and 4.133). At the same time they were the group most likely to post strongly sentimental messages and images that relate to close family relationships, especially to their own children (Figs 4.134 and 4.135). They are also more likely to show tattoos of their children (Figs 4.136 and 4.137). Finally they are the group most likely to post more sentimental messages around gender relations. These may in certain cases reflect the sometimes troubled nature of those relationships (Fig. 4.138).

As is usually the case in such reportage, a chapter that tries to locate the normative is based on generalisation. It was important to include sections on posts both by those who identify with homosexuality and by those in this separated-out class fraction because such posts are anomalous with regards to wider trends in posting, which will be explored further in Chapter 6 as a generic 'Englishness' of posting. But we could then break up those categories further. The female and male gay examples were entirely different from each other in how they represented homosexuality on Facebook. Indeed, this is one of the few cases in this book where the exemplification of differences has come down

Women living in social housing are more likely to refer directly to sex and to their own financial circumstances

These women are also more likely to post sentimental memes about their core relationships

Posting tattoos referencing one's children was a genre found only in this community

There are also memes asserting clear gendered values

to the contrast between two individuals. Throughout this book, however, we try to recognise that our task is to explore normative and typical genres which hold for most people in the field sites, while continuing to acknowledge that no particular individual need accord with local or other stereotypes; there is always room for exceptions and atypical behaviour. This is especially important to bear in mind when we come to general issues of English and Trinidadian postings in Chapters 6 and 7.

5
Trinidadian adults

Chapter 3 found both overlaps and significant differences between the ways people in El Mirador and The Glades become constituted as adults. It was suggested that while new mothers in The Glades appear to show a devotion to their identity as parents, those of El Mirador specifically repudiate such a shift and strive to ensure that they maintain a glamorous image uninterrupted by motherhood. Indeed, both glamour and looking good remain important to women even when they are elderly. This is not viewed as vanity, but rather a duty to oneself and others.[1] The underlying reasons behind this in terms of people's concepts of identity and truth will be explored further in Chapter 7.

Looking good is a general goal shared by the people of El Mirador – but as people become adults the contexts in which they appear start to gain greater significance. This may include both institutional frames, such as the world of work, and cultural frames of social class and ethnicity. In his ethnography of work in Trinidad, Yelvington argues that class, gender and ethnicity are integral aspects to what you see in another person. In Trinidad people see each other as 'having' a class, a gender and an ethnicity.[2] One of the advantages of studying social media – and especially of examining visual posting – is that we as academics can literally see how these are visually expressed.

We noted earlier that the world of work, which one might expect to be central to becoming an adult, is almost entirely absent from postings in The Glades, at least when used as a setting for photographs of people. By contrast images of people at work are of considerable importance to the inhabitants of El Mirador. What matters is not so much the kind of work a person does, however, as the adoption of a dress code that signifies a respectable job and a working person. Work and dressing for work establishes how class is expressed on Facebook. By contrast, gender is often established more through posts that are comments about the nature of gender relationships: either positive ideals of romantic relationships or comments on the antagonistic relationship between the genders. This chapter finishes with a discussion on ethnicity – a complex scenario, as in Trinidad ethnicity is not simply a series of fixed categories. These visual postings will be used to show how some aspects of stereotyping of Indo-Trinidadians and Afro-Trinidadians are also appropriated by the other.

Work and home

Following completion of high school, young people and parents alike pay considerable attention to what they wear to work. Appendix Figure 1 shows that 343 images were taken at work or related places in El Mirador, but only 12 in The Glades. Appendix Figure 4 shows that people in the two sites equally post about work as a topic, so the difference concerns situating people in the work context. In Trinidad photos posted from the workplace are especially important for establishing upward mobility.[3] For professionals who have fairly secure jobs and mobility within the private sector, photos taken at work are more playful and casual; they can include selfies or photos of colleagues or their vocation. But otherwise dressing up for work and looking good emerges as a serious concern in profile pictures (Figs 5.1, 5.2 and 5.3).

The act of dressing for work is here just as appropriate a subject for a selfie as dressing for going out in the evening. Dressing for work is an expensive business, since there is an ideal of not wearing the same outfit twice at work unless the person has to wear a uniform. So it is likely that this degree of expense and effort is being reflected through such Facebook postings.

For young people just starting out on their careers, university graduates or lower income individuals looking to expand their opportunities, showing enthusiasm about their work through facial expression and demonstrating professionalism through body language and dress is important. Posting images with work colleagues is another genre of posts that create social acknowledgement and build relationships and collegiality (Figs 5.4 and 5.5).

Photos of work parties and 'limes' (a Trinidadian term for going out, see below) are also frequently posted, as are associated travel and conferences: all serve to emphasise the individual's skills and merits as well as the achievements of the group. Work trips contain similar elements to everyday posts – liming, parties, drinks and food – but

Showing work outfits is important for cultivating a professional-looking profile

Images taken by colleagues show collegiality and create social acknowledgement

Images of socialising with colleagues on foreign trips, especially in exotic locations, portray a glamorous lifestyle underlying work events

ideally at more up-market, glamorous or exotic (that is, distant) settings (Figs 5.6 and 5.7).

Most work dress is strictly formal, consisting of suits for men or shirts and trousers. Women wear tailored dresses or fitted, knee-length skirts with tapered shirts or blouses. Footwear is made of leather and is fitted, and hair is neat and styled back, off the face. Casualness in dress, or any kind of unkemptness, is a sign of poor upbringing or of being from a lower class, so there are rarely photos of people looking sloppy or with their clothes just thrown together. Most Trinidadians simply would not leave the house in such informal dress if they were going anywhere beyond a relative's home. Respectability can be demonstrated both through how one dresses and through the company one keeps, as shown in these photos of work-related events. The emphasis is as much on the social relations of work as on the experience of the job and the act of working itself (Fig. 5.8).[4]

This genre of work clothing is further reinforced by a striking contrast with the leisure environment of home (Figs 5.9 and 5.10). Here people may go to the opposite extreme and post images of themselves wearing shorts, T-shirts and flip-flops, though men rarely go as far as posting images of themselves 'bare back' (without a shirt). Women will wear sloppy shirts or tank tops, short or shapeless skirts, but again only up to a certain level of informality.

Social relations at work are shown as much as vocations

A trend in Facebook cover photos in El Mirador is to display the company or place you work for, especially if it is a small business. These complement or contrast with profile pictures, which emphasise either

Photos showing very casual clothes worn within the home

attractiveness, sociability or the person's professional persona. Cover images can look corporate and professional or colourful, especially for people who work in restaurants or bars (Figs 5.11 and 5.12).

For workers in small or family-run businesses, posting on Facebook is often a side effect of boredom. Men tend to share more humorous memes, while women will experiment with hair and make-up on particularly quiet days and post more 'boredom selfies'; both share statuses, likes and, to a lesser extent, comment on posts. Trinidadians rarely get into serious discussion or commentary on Facebook unless they strongly identify with an issue or identify with being an activist. This is out of fear of ostracisation, blocking or a feeling of putting oneself out there too much. Instead work posts focus upon mood, humour and style.

Young women often post images of themselves doing their make-up or experimenting with hairstyles that again may reflect boredom. This is common not only for people who work in salons or are beauticians, but also for those who work in clothes or shoe stores where there

Cover images may include a business one owns or where one is employed

Examples of young women's posts during working hours

can be extensive periods with no customers. They often form groups of Facebook friends who thereby help to occupy each other's time in the reciprocity of likes and comments (Figs 5.13, 5.14 and 5.15).

Adding comments to photos which link the post to boredom is also a way of legitimising good-looking photos of oneself without appearing to be too self-regarding. Such images can attract dozens of likes and several comments (Figs 5.16a and 5.16b).

Posting an attractive image attributed to boredom appears less self-regarding (a). In this case it drew many favourable comments (b)

Images of the family also include extended family, in contrast to the English field site

If we now turn to the examination of images set in the home, the emphasis shifts – not to the home itself, which is rarely the subject of a posting, but rather to its role as a setting for relationships to the wider family, a theme already developed during childhood and adolescence. Also, as previously, images with the extended family are as prominent as those showing the immediate family (Figs 5.17 and 5.18).

For formal occasions, such as weddings, graduations, anniversaries, work functions and Hindu *pujas* (prayers), poses are as formal as the attire. People line up and stand in groups, place their hands in front of them or by their sides and pose with a neutral expression or a slight smile. In Appendix Figure 2 we find 19 out of the 50 people sampled for their profile pictures show people dressed in more formal wear for an event (with a total of 70 such photos), compared to only a single such case in The Glades – formality on the English site is often viewed as opposed to authenticity, and thereby seen as less appropriate for a profile picture. In El Mirador formal occasion photos seem to replicate the formal portraiture that in the past was more characteristic of official or bureaucratic documentation (Figs 5.19 and 5.20).

In photos of the family and family events, gender seems less important as a category, with little posing in overtly feminine or masculine forms (Fig. 5.21). Nor is there much sense of individual style, beyond looking appropriate for the occasion and looking respectable. This is also secondary to the importance of the image as capturing a sense of occasion.

Gender

In The Glades, the expression of gender gender consists largely of the establishment of genres of postings. For females this might be memes themed around 'girls out together', or an association with wine or

Poses in photos of formal occasions resemble formal portraiture from the past

In photos of family groups, posing in overtly masculine or feminine forms is rare

dieting; for males this might be photos of football and beer. We find equivalents of these in El Mirador, but an equally important element is more direct commentary on gender relationships. First, however, we need to examine how both masculinity and femininity are established as visual styles.

For lower middle-class and lower income populations in El Mirador, we find an identification with the 'gangsta' image evident in US hip-hop culture. For young men, young gangsta masculinity includes wearing caps, low-hanging oversized jeans, trainers, T-shirts or singlets that emphasise their upper body, gold chains, watches and sunglasses (Figs 5.22, 5.23 and 5.24). In Appendix Figure 4 we find hats and caps appearing in 254 photographs in El Mirador, compared with just 52 in The Glades. Young men who subscribe to the 'gangsta' image also post photos of money, memes about money or making money and images of conspicuous consumption, such as expensive drinks and posing with expensive cars (Figs 5.25, 5.26 and 5.27). The adoption of the 'gangsta' image is popular with young men who see themselves as identifying with the intersections

Some young men adopt the 'gangsta' image from US hip-hop culture

Young men who adopt the gangsta image also post about money and making money

of race, class, gender and sexuality that are embodied stylistically in hip-hop culture.[5]

Young men also post photos with several different young women at clubs or on nights out. It is difficult to tell from the photographs whether these young men are in serious relationships or not. Posts that show how they can attract a variety of women intriguingly share the walls with quite different posts in which these same males want to appear sincere, sensitive and trustworthy to attract women with the promise of genuine, longer-term relationships.

There are also men who concentrate on wanting to be seen as more rounded or more genuine, who are either in more permanent relationships or who are seeking them. They largely post images associated with work, where they went on vacation and their friends (Figs 5.28 and 5.29).

In terms of wider interests, young men continue to post about gaming and sport, especially associated with events such as the World Cup, but to a far lesser extent than teenage boys (Figs 5.30, 5.31 and 5.32). Working men, although they may play sports or train recreationally, don't display the intensive competition and time investment in sports achievements found with teenage boys. Professional men may post motivational posts associated with work and success as well as

Men who wish to be seen as more professional post about work and leisure

Young men post about interests such as the World Cup or gaming, but to a lesser extent than teenagers

images of themselves at work-related events, dressed very professionally (Figs 5.33, 5.34, 5.35 and 5.36).

In El Mirador, postings of young women suggest a subtle ambivalence towards aligning with gender norms. On the one hand, there is an emphasis on being independent and having their own means. While they rarely post about their interests, young women are happy to emphasise a lifestyle based on their taste and aesthetic appreciation. At the same time, although these images might not be explicitly linked to trying to attract a man, there remains a clear concern only to post images in which they look good. Consequently photos of everyday wear, being around work, going out and socialising all retain a focus on their looks (Figs. 5.37, 5.38 and 5.39). As noted, the primary difference between The Glades and El Mirador is that while people in both field sites use visual posts which portray gender as the separate norms of masculinity and femininity, there are far more comments upon the general state of gender relations in El Mirador[6] in the form of memes. Appendix Figures 2 and 4 suggest that memes are about three times as likely to be posted in El Mirador as in The Glades, both in regular postings and as profile pictures. Furthermore, while those in The Glades are mainly humorous, in El Mirador funny memes are complemented by moral and serious posts, mostly commenting on the nature of relationships. There is often also an element of religiosity in memes about romantic relationships, although religious memes also appear as their own genre (see Chapter 7). This

Professional men also post images of themselves at work events and motivational memes

Images posted by young women emphasise lifestyle, attractiveness and independence

religious component is found in postings by people of any religion. The longer the relationship progresses, the less the person puts up posts of this kind; instead we start to see more photos of couples together and examples of courtship.

These serious memes with their moral commentaries about romantic relationships and love generally argue that romantic love should also mean fidelity, loyalty, trust, sensitivity and care (Figs 5.40, 5.41, 5.42 and 5.43). Even the more humorous memes about gender roles and expectations may carry underlying currents concerned with issues of neglect, being taken for granted emotionally and, sometimes, the hint of abusive relationships (Figs 5.44, 5.45, 5.46 and 5.47).

There is often a considerable ambivalence in these postings regarding two tensions within relationships. Firstly, they favour a committed relationship, but also emphasise the importance of being able to retain one's autonomy in a relationship and not be taken for granted.[7] Secondly, they express an idealistic (through moralising) view about relationships,

Memes are widely used to give moral commentary about the ideal state of gender relationships

5.41
It's not always about sex, sometimes the best type of intimacy is where you just lay back, laugh together at the stupidest things, hold each other, and enjoy each others company...

5.40

The relationship between a husband and wife should be like the relationship between the hand and the eye. If the hand gets hurt the eye cries and if the eye cries, the hand wipes its tears. ♡

5.42

If you wouldn't make her a wife.

Don't make her a mother.

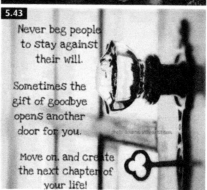

5.43
Never beg people to stay against their will.

Sometimes the gift of goodbye opens another door for you.

Move on. and create the next chapter of your life!

More humorous memes also
have undercurrents indicating
some of the negative aspects of
relationships

but also identify, usually through humour, the generalised antagonistic view that each gender holds of the other.

Class

Class in Trinidad has a complex history and is heavily entwined with race relations.[8] Singh argues that in the first 50 years, post-emancipation, ex-enslaved Africans who were clearly unable to compete with the white upper class in terms of holding property tried to attain status through education and cultural capital.[9] Generally, by contrast, ex-indentured East Indians sought to hold land and to generate wealth through business and entrepreneurship. Historically, there were various ways to make wealth and status visible, which included overt signs of achievement in education and the embracing of British and American culture, as well as adorning the home and oneself in acquired material things – all themes that run through V. S. Naipaul's fictional writings on Trinidad.[10]

In El Mirador discussions around class that come out in everyday conversations are mainly expressed through the use of the terms 'stush' and 'ghetto', which describe among other things the aesthetics of clothes and taste, and how people behave at celebrations or fetes. Both terms are coloured by moral judgements beyond simply describing being rich or poor: 'stush' implies that not only does one have money and better, or more elite, taste, but that one thinks one is better than other people because of these things. 'Ghetto' implies the opposite – that one has cheap, tacky and flamboyant taste, is loud and brash and has a crude sense of sexuality. 'Ghetto' also has a negative racial element that is often used offensively to describe lower income Afro-Trinidadians. The people who are the targets of being called 'ghetto' sometimes resist their positioning by overtly ascribing to the stereotype in order make others uncomfortable. 'Ghetto' can also be used to be extremely offensive, in the same manner that 'nigger' was used historically. In El Mirador, however, the term 'nigger' may cause even less offence than 'ghetto'.

This is because Trinidadian racial epithets are entirely different from those of the US, with terms such as 'coolie' and 'nigger' remaining part of everyday greetings for decades after they became unacceptable in the US. Today, however, some people have re-appropriated the US inflected term 'nigga' instead – precisely an example of how people who find themselves branded as 'ghetto' respond by incorporating terms that make 'stush' people uncomfortable. As we show later in the chapter, 'nigga' also continues to be used more humorously, without the political and racial implications of 'ghetto'.

The sense of class is increasingly linked to the idea of cosmopolitanism in Trinidad. In the last couple of years, with the introduction of 3G and with WiFi broadband more readily available in homes, we see a new trend among women in their early twenties who are university educated and young professionals of different ethnic backgrounds. While the images that they post retain some of the genres that we've already discussed, including the concern with pose and sexuality, they increasingly display influences that can be described as more 'global.' This may include images posted of food alone, dishes at American chain restaurants or restaurants in malls, holidays to other Caribbean islands or further abroad, clothes and make-up (Figs 5.48 and 5.49). These young women follow fashion blogs avidly; they bookmark them, subscribe to them on YouTube and experiment with looks they've seen from bloggers who exhibit fashion in the US, the UK and Asia, most notably, Singapore.

Young women also post more 'global' genres, such as images of food alone or restaurants

The fashion or lifestyle bloggers, make-up and style gurus they follow on YouTube defy the image of the 'all-American girl' that was popularised in Trinidad with Hannah Montana.[11] For women in their early twentiess, the social media icons they follow have their own sense of 'glocality' – global images that can be appropriated in multiple local sites. As such, these are women to whom Trinidadians feel that they can relate. Popular social media style icons are from countries with similar histories and cultures to Trinidad: places with multiple ethnic backgrounds, with a colonial past and a growing middle class. Most of the bloggers are the same age as their followers, in their late twenties or early thirties, and generally their blogs emphasise beauty, consumption and lifestyle. Very few of the bloggers these young women follow write about sexual relationships or romance tips; instead they post about being close to one's family and others values with which young Trinidadian women can identify.

A core component in the expression of class through postings is that associated with travel and mobility. Most Trinidadians in El Mirador will have taken a holiday in their sister island of Tobago. Images from Tobago, as well as beaches and nature leisure spots around Trinidad, are common, often focused upon relatives and friends having a good time (Figs 5.50 and 5.51).

For the more upwardly mobile, male and female, travel images may emphasise more exotic or distant locations (Figs 5.52 and 5.53).

Typical settings are Florida, New York, the UK or other Caribbean islands (Figs 5.54 and 5.55). Frequency and distance of travel are an important indicator of social class within Trinidad. Instagram collages are popular with the young middle class in the capital, but, since the platform was rare in El Mirador at the time of this research, it is not being considered here.

Going to the beach and other nature leisure spots are popular weekend activities

International travel is enjoyed by the more upwardly mobile

Trips further abroad are indicative of having a higher income

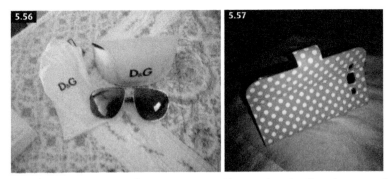

Framing expensive items as gifts is a more acceptable way of posting these images, as it avoids being seen as showing off

While materialism and consumption can be reflected in photographic posting, people who consider themselves to be of higher classes want to maintain their sophisticated image. Conscious that they could appear crass or vulgar by posting images of consumption, one strategy is to frame expensive items as gifts from others, rather than crudely showing off 'this is what I bought' (Figs 5.56 and 5.57).

The contrast is with people from lower income groups. They might more directly associate themselves with branded goods, but more as part of popular culture which includes also associations with films, television and music. Appendix Figure 1 shows that branded goods are evident in 147 images from El Mirador, but in only six images from The Glades. Appendix Figure 4 shows the last 20 postings included only nine foreign music videos posted by seven people in the Glades, as compared with 125 videos posted by 36 people in El Mirador – though this obviously also reflects the relative size of the local music industry. US music videos, especially associated with hip-hop and Top 40 songs, are generally popular in Trinidad, as are more sentimental or love songs from the 1980s to now. Often the latter include comments such as 'an oldie but so true', or 'still true', or 'a classic'. This sharing of music links and videos is common to teenagers and young adults and declines with age (Figs 5.58 and 5.59).

People from peripheral areas such as El Mirador often post images that relate to time spent in the fashionable areas of Port of Spain, though lower income groups would probably visit less frequently (Figs 5.60 and 5.61). For the middle class this might include postings of restaurant and bar food, where the emphasis is on dining and presentation.

Posts of food from lower income groups are also common, but the types of food posted are more likely taken from cooking with family and friends, takeaways or beach and river cook-ups (Figs 5.62 and 5.63).

Sharing music videos expresses emotions or mood, and is particularly popular among teenagers and young adults

People living in more peripheral areas enjoy visits to the sophisticated city of Port of Spain

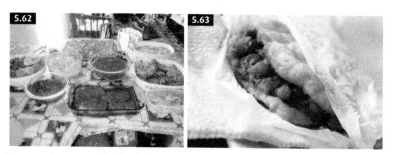

Other popular posts of food include take-away meals and dishes prepared at home

In addition, while middle-class women will post popular local food, they also present what they perceive to be cosmopolitan foods, where the emphasis is not on the company or the occasion, but on the status of the food itself. An example occurs in Chapter 8 where one of the images, that of focaccia bread, promotes a food that most Trinidadians would not have heard of.

Trinidadians in El Mirador generally post more about food than the English in The Glades. This could be explained partly by the way these posts on food reflect class, but also the importance of food and eating to socialising associated with 'liming' (see Chapter 7). Appendix Figure 1 shows that in the posting of visual images there are 126 photos of food and people in El Mirador, compared with only 79 in The Glades. In addition, food alone appears in 253 photos compared to 65 in The Glades.

Differentiation is also important in images of drinks. More elaborate drinks, such as cocktails or shots of liqueur, are shown alone or in bars where the background is clearly visible and reflects middle-class lifestyles. Multiple empty beer bottles that show how much has been drunk and spirit bottles are more common to lower middle-class posting. Alcohol brands that would be recognised in Trinidad as expensive are posted regardless of people's incomes (Figs 5.64, 5.65, 5.66 and 5.67).

Expensive alcohol brands are posted regardless of level of income, as alcohol is considered important for showing enjoyment as well as lifestyle

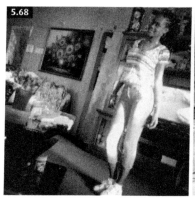

Images of home interiors can indicate a middle-class status

If food is more common in El Mirador posting than in The Glades, the opposite is true for drinks; these feature in 352 photos in El Mirador, but in 568 images posted in The Glades. The difference reflects the earlier discussion about how the English, most notably teenagers, need to show a drink in their hands to indicate that they are having a good time.

Photos of home interiors rarely focus on the furnishing, though as backgrounds they certainly mark a contrast between middle-class homes (Figs 5.68 and 5.69) and lower income ones (Figs 5.70 and 5.71).

Even when Miller carried out his initial field work in Trinidad in 1988, cars were strikingly important as an expression of individual taste and identity.[12] At that time cars, as much as homes and clothes, were heavily adorned and accessorised, and people put a large amount of

Lower income homes are shown as unfinished, such as needing a coat of paint or still being in the process of completion

Cars remain powerful emblems of a high-class lifestyle and aspirations

time, effort and expense into maintaining them. Today almost all cars appear washed and shiny, with around half also showing wider elaboration and decorative work. This might range from religious motifs to fancy lights, or hubcaps and wheels made up to resemble those of racing cars.

On social media people may pose with cars, as emblems of a high-class lifestyle, or to suggest going out to have fun (Figs 5.72, 5.73 and 5.74).

In addition people, especially those in their early twenties, may show off the cars themselves – either in their entirety or through a focus on specific parts such as modified doors, wheels, decoration or other features. There is no equivalent in The Glades, where cars are always in the background rather than a focal point (Figs 5.75, 5.76 and 5.77).

Ethnicity

Trinidad has a mixed population. It includes approximately 35 per cent who are descended from indentured East Indians (from south Asia) and 35 per cent who are descended from ex-enslaved Africans. The remaining 30 per cent are descended from Chinese, South American, Syrian, Lebanese and European (locally termed French Creole, irrespective of which part of Europe they originated from) and mixed backgrounds. Khan (2004) describes Trinidad as a 'callaloo' society – the name of a national dish in which different vegetables are boiled, then blended together to make one dish. Diversity is also expressed in religion – not just between Hindus, Muslims and Christians, but sometimes through highly significant differences between their respective denominations,

Cars are popular subjects of posts, either in their entirety or parts that have been modified, which is rarely found in The Glades

for example Pentecostal and Catholic Christians. Trinidadians have developed a number of ways to show that they belong to different categories of ethnicity and religion; these are worn and shown on the body,[13] a practice that now extends to social media.

When it comes to ethnicity, however, social media also reflects Trinidad's long history of co-existence, meaning that today each group is comfortable posting images originating from groups outside of their own. A good example of this is the way in which the gangsta aesthetic (see above) can today be found equally among Indo-Trinidadian and Afro-Trinidadian men. Young adults show themselves with others of both backgrounds, commonly referring to each other in banter as 'nigga' or 'dawg' and, to a lesser extent, 'coolie'. Racial epithets are used openly in El Mirador and don't cause offence if they are used between friends or with humour, although they still have the potential to be used in a derogatory way for the denigration of others (Figs 5.78 and 5.79).

Young women also post featuring the word 'nigga', which again can be friendly and humorous in certain contexts. However, it also extends to a more derogatory usage, usually when talking about men they consider obnoxious (Fig. 5.80).

Racial epithets are used openly between friends, particularly in a humorous context

Young women appropriate the word 'nigga', which can be friendly or derogatory

Afro-centrism is more unequivocally positive when manifested through Rastafarian culture, particularly in the appearance of Bob Marley in posts. These include merchandise such as T-shirts, visiting iconic sites and posting song quotes or images (Figs 5.81, 5.82 and 5.83). The Rastafarian culture embodied by Marley is embraced by Afro-Trinidadians and Indo-Trinidadians alike.

East Indian cultural heritage is mostly visible through clothes for religious or family events such as Hindu prayers (*pujas*), weddings and anniversaries. Both men and women take pride in styling themselves for these events and post photos taken before leaving the house and at the event itself (Figs 5.84 and 5.85). Once again, however, extended families often incorporate mixed Indo-Afro nuclear families, so there would often be at least one relative of another ethnic background present. Today it is also common that at Indian family events there would also be mixed or Afro-Trinidadians

Afro-centrism is embraced through Rastafarian culture embodied by Bob Marley

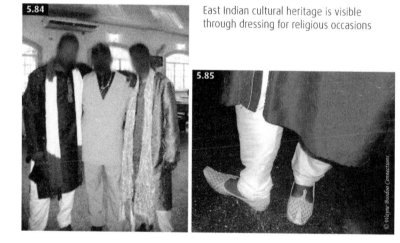

East Indian cultural heritage is visible through dressing for religious occasions

wearing Indian ethnic clothing. The incorporation of visual images therefore goes in both directions (Figs 5.86, 5.87, 5.88 and 5.89).

Within these more general ethnic categories, there remains a subtler positioning based on traits such as precise skin colour, build and the texture of hair. Liking Facebook pages around hair is also a common mode for expressing ethnic heritage (Fig. 5.90).

Trinidadians have a rich vocabulary of terms related to mixed heritage such as 'red', which means having some European ancestry,

Indian ethnic clothing is worn on special occasions by those of different backgrounds

Ethnic heritage can also appear through 'liking' pages dedicated to styling, such as hair

Siblings of mixed heritages can look quite different, and their experiences can vary depending on appearance

or 'dougla', referring to mixed Indo-Trinidadian and Afro-Trinidadian. The continued significance of these differences is most evident from the cases of siblings in mixed families. The sibling who looks more African may have very different experiences from the one who looks more Indian (Figs 5.91 and 5.92).

Some people's posts make explicit their claims to cultural heritage, for example through the way they post images of 'African' hair and hairstyles. Others avoid such positioning by posting more 'global' influences around lifestyle, consumption and interests such as vacations abroad.

Other minorities are also present. When we look at posts of recent Chinese migrants in El Mirador, we see a contrast, not only in content – here humour, memes and an emphasis on looks are rarely posted – but also in how the Chinese relate to China as their homeland. Chinese migration in Trinidad goes back to labourers arriving in the post-emancipation years of the 1850s.[14] More recent migration from the 1990s, however, reflects China's new involvement in the global economy.[15] The handful of Chinese in El Mirador who are on Facebook migrated to the area in 2010. They own and work in Chinese restaurants and have extended family in Trinidad. As with the rural migrants to factory towns studied within our project by Wang, they display their attachment to their home villages in 'homeland' albums, posted on the Chinese social media platform QQ.[16] In El Mirador young female Chinese migrants also post about their friends at home in China through albums called 'I Miss You' or 'Memory' (Figs 5.93 and 5.94).

Their posts emphasise the difficulty of living and working away from their homeland. Life in El Mirador is characterised by long hours working in the restaurant, with Sunday as their only day off (Fig. 5.95). Although several have settled permanently in Trinidad, these posts reflect what Liu describes as *huaqiao* – Chinese sojourners who consider themselves to only be living overseas temporarily, and whose cultural

Recent Chinese migrants express their attachment to home by posting groups of photos forming 'homeland' albums

Other posts emphasise their migrant experience of living and working away from home

Although they have migrated to Trinidad, Chinese migrants' cultural orientation remains towards China

orientation is still towards China (Fig. 5.96).[17] This is similar to the situation of Filipina maids who 'lived' in London, but whose orientation remained to their homeland.[18]

While this section has concentrated upon ethnicity as difference, perhaps the most surprising content showed a degree of cross incorporation especially between Afro-Trinidadians and Indo-Trinidadians.

This leads on to a consideration in Chapter 7 of quite a strong sense of 'Trini-ness', in which ethnicity becomes subservient to a wider national identity.

Conclusion

This chapter has focused on several parameters of differentiated identity as they are rendered visible through postings on Facebook. On the one hand, there are personal relationships to nuclear and extended family, and those developed through friendships. On the other hand, social structures also create various sets of affinity that people negotiate, set around class, gender and ethnicity as well as work. These relationships and structures emerge more clearly in the posts of adults rather than teenagers. The groundwork is laid by young people experimenting with styles, identity and association with others. For adults, however, these become more fixed and normative categories of identity that are taken for granted as who they now are.

The chapter began by looking at the role and importance of relationships to people, the expectations and obligations around friendship, family and romantic relationships through memes, status updates and commentary and the direct portrayal of relationships on Facebook. It then shifted from personal relationships to focus on the workplace, working life appearing just as prominently in profiles and posts as do friends and family. This emphasis upon work in El Mirador strongly contrasts with the lack of any such association in The Glades – part of a more general contrast that will be analysed more deeply over the next two chapters. Postings about work were also found to be central to the establishment of class identity in Trinidad. Carried through into consumption, class may also be expressed through cultural capital found in the aesthetic appreciation of cosmopolitan food and drink.[19] We also see class proclaimed through travel destinations, from weekend and beach outings to more remote destinations and holiday photos that signify higher incomes and more opportunities.

Consumption and image are strongly linked to gender. More international or global styles signify independence and choice for women just as much as the gangsta image represents independence and reputation for men. For lower-middle-class and lower-income people, portrayal of lifestyle is less common than posting around relationships, whether time spent with others or moral commentary on the expectations of relationships through the posting of moralising memes. As people move upwards in terms of income, they post less about the moral state of relationships and more around lifestyle and consumption.

Class, gender and ethnicity in Trinidad have been treated within this chapter as sequential topics with their own particular characteristics. This will shift dramatically when we come to Chapter 7. There we will argue that all of these social parameters not only map on to each other – each also expresses a wider and more foundational dualism that we will refer to as the values of transience and transcendence. Being a man, but also being Afro-Trinidadian and lower class can together come to embody reputation, the world of the street and what is temporary. In contrast women, while also being, for example, Indo-Trinidadian and higher class, embody respectability, the home and what is permanent.

6
The Englishness of posting

The argument of this chapter is fairly simple: while Trinidadian values, as presented through the visual postings from El Mirador, are based on a dualism of two extremes – what we will call transience and transcendence – the values of the English, as seen from visual posts in The Glades, seem to be all about cultivating the middle ground and avoiding any such extremes. So this chapter will examine how postings are used to characterise a suburban ethos, starting from the domestication of dogs and cats. We will then argue that this middle ground is protected and established through two main mechanisms, the first being self-effacement and modesty and the second humour. The chapter will end at the point where these two meet in that most English of English genres – self-deprecating humour.

Cats and dogs

One of the striking things about the way English people post their cats and dogs is that the language is often reminiscent of the way in which they refer to babies and toddlers. One reason for this may simply be that pets sometimes substitute for infants. There is some evidence that this has been an English tradition that may go back to the sixteenth century.[1] Some young couples seem to adopt pets as a sort of 'practice baby', giving an exaggerated attention to the welfare of their pet that is constantly being monitored. Older people may have pets when their children have left home, or in the absence of much interaction with grandchildren. This was very clear in one instance where the family had dispersed and it had become quite rare to get visits from the grandchildren – here a lively dog seemed to do the job pretty well.

However, there is another quality that comes across perhaps more strongly in these postings. Considered in their role as Facebook postings, toddlers and pets have a very important characteristic in common – in both cases the subjects are incapable of posting for themselves. This means that the person who is doing the posting is free to post pretty much anything they like as purporting to come from the infant or pet. This makes both toddlers and pets ideal conduits for projecting ourselves vicariously through another living being. Such a situation may in turn explain why there is so much elision between the two genres of posting, as made unusually explicit in this image (Fig. 6.1).

Just as with posting of infants, we often start with the naked vulnerability of the animal (Figs 6.2 and 6.3).

An alternative may show young pets wearing clothing made to look like animal 'babygrows', or in least infantalising them (Figs 6.4 and 6.5).

The fact that one of these photographs features quite a fearsome husky is perhaps indicative of this process. With cats, images often seem to express an ideal of domestic containment (Figs 6.6 and 6.7).

The explicit anthropomorphising of the relationship as one of parenting or grandparenting is reinforced in accompanying texts. Photographs of animals may be referred to with comments such as

There are clear parallels between pets and children in the way adults can pose them in order to express the values they project on to them

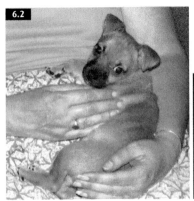

Pets, as babies, can be used to show how adults provide them with security

Pets can also be infantilised through dressing, which also allows them to be treated as an accessory

Cats can be used to express domestic containment

'mummy's little helper', 'having a cuddle', 'it's cuddle time', 'on mummy's knee' or 'helping with the knitting' (Figs 6.8 and 6.9). Alternatives are commands with a humorous note: 'Stop playing with that laptop and FEED ME!!" There can also be a collusion around 'being a child' in the combination of photograph and caption, for instance 'I don't know who is naughtier, Derek or me for eating ice cream in bed' (Fig. 6.10) and 'My poor little baby is hopefully on the mend' (Fig. 6.11).

Captions for images with pets often show parallels to parenting

The fullest expression of this domestication is that even breeds of dogs such as Alsatians, perceived in Trinidad as the ultimate guard dogs of the street, are in The Glades typically posted lying on the owner's bed (Figs 6.12 and 6.13). Cats also commonly feature on beds (Figs 6.14 and 6.15) and both cats and dogs appear on sofas (Figs 6.16 and 6.17). People in The Glades posted 100 photographs of dogs versus 52 in El Mirador (Appendix Figure 1). While there are 32 cat

When a pet suffers an illness or injury, the child–parent parallel becomes even stronger

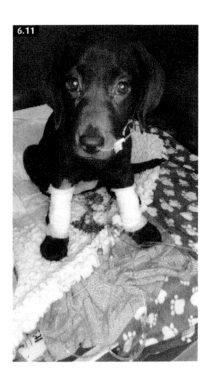

Pets are often described as being 'naughty'

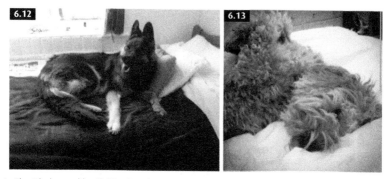

In The Glades, unlike El Mirador, dogs are more often shown inside, even on the owner's bed

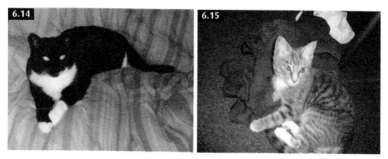

Cats also appear on beds

photographs in El Mirador compared to 36 in The Glades, 20 of those in El Mirador are posted by the same person (Appendix Figure 1). However, the important contrast comes when we examine how the animals are viewed. It is striking that at least on Facebook (Instagram is different), approximately 90 per cent of photographs of cats and 80 per cent of photographs of dogs are taken *inside* the home rather than outside. This is despite the fact that The Glades is a village with abundant opportunity to go walking in the fields. Dog owners are often to be seen in certain well-known areas at the periphery of the village; these shared walking areas are one of the places where the animals become a means of developing friendships between owners. Yet pets are rarely posted on Facebook while on these walks, as compared to lying on carpets and sofas. By contrast we will see in Chapter 8 that to post a photo of a dog inside is so exceptional that most people commenting on the image simply assumed that it could not actually be a Trinidadian doing the posting.

Both cats and dogs appear on couches

Even the outside shots of animals can look pretty domesticated. If dogs do appear outside on Facebook, it is most likely because they are on holiday or going for long walks. In such images they appear as an accompaniment to English people's enjoyment of long country walks (Figs 6.18 and 6.19).

In addition some young girls have a 'horse phase', with the ability to indulge this being seen as a perk of living in a village (Fig. 6.20).

So although photos of dogs and cats are both posted in El Mirador and The Glades, in the former they are creatures of the outside world

Even the outside shots emphasise dogs in pretty environments or on a lead rather than fearsome or strong

Young girls often have a 'horse' phase which they like to post on Facebook

Other images reinforce the sense of the dog as a domesticated animal rather than one kept for security, in contrast to El Mirador

and the street, while in The Glades they are part of a more general project of domestication (Fig. 6.21). Another image portrays a dog engaging with the weather – perhaps the single most favoured topic of English domestic life (Fig. 6.22). The amusing context is reinforced by the accompanying text.

In the section on humour, we will start to differentiate between these pets. In contrast to 'man's best friend', the cat is regarded as the more naturally autonomous – and can consequently be used to express a more ambivalent commentary on this domestic bliss.

'Checking out the weather before going out for a walk'

Suburbia

Pets in England have become an extreme example of taking originally wild forms and turning them into, in this case, accoutrements of the bedroom, or members of the family analogous to toddlers. This domestication reflects a wider set of ideals in England; values that are most fully expressed by the concept of suburbia. Suburbia is itself a highly consistent expression of English values, fully embodied by The Glades – a dual village that is able to encompass all that English people expect of village life and yet has rapid access to everything that London has to offer. This combination of the best of town and country might have been achieved by a similar dualism to that we find in Trinidad – one that kept each pole as integral and opposed. But instead in The Glades we found a constant focus upon that which combines the two. Suburbia is best expressed by the semantic continuity of the half-timbered, semi-detached, sub-urban areas of the middle class.

Returning for a moment to those dogs; currently the main passion that is found among The Glades dog owners is for new forms of dogs – a rather neat expression of this consistent search for the compromise or middle group. The true dogs of The Glades are now the Cockapoos and the Labradoodles, which were far and away the breeds of dogs most commonly discussed by informants in the village. Both represent the deliberate interbreeding of a traditional sporting and field dog with a miniature or toy dog that is particularly resonant of this domesticity. It is hard to imagine how the English could have more clearly expressed this cultivation of suburbia through selective breeding.

The same argument seems to carry for another major genre of posting. It would have been perfectly possible for the people of The Glades to post streams of photographs of the fields and forests that lie just beyond the village and are extremely scenic. Equally they might have posted abundant images of their home interiors, to which they devote considerable time and attention. While photographs can be found of both of these, they are actually quite rare on Facebook. People do not point their camera at the inside of a room to show off their decoration unless it has been newly done up for an infant or unless they wish to illustrate some labour in the tradition of DIY. The latter, a consummately suburban pastime, is significantly mainly shown when it has gone wrong and is therefore amusing (Fig. 6.23).

The iconic activity of suburbia, home improvements are usually only shown on Facebook when they have gone wrong

The one genre that does seem well suited to showing suburban values, because it is neither pure country nor home interior, is the garden. We found 48 photos of domestic gardens in The Glades, but none at all in El Mirador, where shots of home interiors are more common than in The Glades. This is reminiscent of the experience of the Swiss anthropologist Sophie Chevalier, who came to England in the 1990s hoping to replicate her study of French home interiors with English ones. In the end she wrote her paper about gardens because she kept finding that her English informants would rapidly insist that they leave the home area she had come to study and admire the garden outside.[2] The images we find on Facebook feature flowerbeds, paddling pools, the activity of gardening and making snowmen (Figs 6.24, 6.25, 6.26 and 6.27).

The gardens are the place of both labour and relaxation. But this taming process it often represents also goes for the local countryside. Pictures intended as a tribute to the wilderness tend to be located either abroad or in much wilder places, such as the countryside of Scotland. On

People in The Glades are generally fond of posting anything to do with the garden

A popular genre are photographs taken during walks in the countryside

Facebook photos taken in England are more often the results of walking holidays or day trips spent walking in what is often quite a domesticated landscape covered in paths (Fig. 6.28), or scenes of country pubs (Figs 6.29 and 6.30).

The appropriate expression seems to be that of 'cultivating' suburbia. This implies that we cannot take this middle ground for granted: it needs constant protection. The contrast is with the segment of the population discussed at the end of Chapter Four who tend to live in social housing or cheap private rental accommodation. The fact that the postings of that population on topics such as sex and politics are much more vivid and overt may help to define the middle-class sensibility based on a constant desire to distance themselves from these others. Instead they seem to be trying to capture the kind of idyll represented in Tolkien's *The Lord of the Rings* by The Shire: a place that seems secure, but with wolves and orcs beyond its borders. Again we see a stark contrast with El Mirador with its far greater use of images taken from religion, street culture and assertive nationalism.

The study of Facebook postings helps us to identify two key devices that seem to have been appropriated precisely to prevent this movement to extremes. These are forces designed to prevent us from taking ourselves or anything else too seriously, which keep us from climbing up out of the comfortable middle zone. The first of these is simply self-effacement and modesty, ensuring that we do not focus on ourselves as the project, but instead draw attention to the context within which we live. The second mechanism of control is humour – a strategy that tears down any alternative edifice by removing its claims to solidity and seriousness and instead brings us back down to the good earth of the garden.

Self-effacement

One of the striking differences between Trinidad and England is the response of mothers to the birth of their children. The point about the next set of photos is that they are not the profile photos of babies' accounts. They are taken from what are supposed to be the profile photos of their mothers (Figs 6.31 and 6.32).

Far from this being exceptional, it is almost always the case that if you look at the profile picture album of a mother from The Glades on Facebook then the pictures will be a sequence largely of that person – until she gives birth. After the birth and often for a year or two after that point, her profile pictures are more likely to be those of her infant than herself. In some instances she virtually disappears from her own profile pictures.

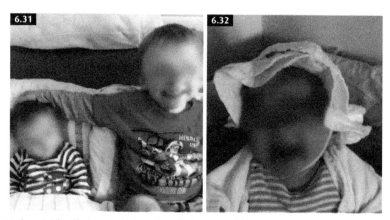

Mothers in The Glades routinely replace their own profile pictures with those of their babies

This illustration is of the entire profile pictures album of one such mother. It starts with an image of her (the oldest images are at the bottom right). After the birth of her child one or two images appear that include both the infant and a parent. After a while she completely disappears, however, to be replaced entirely by the sequential images of the infant alone (Fig. 6.33).

Fathers are more variable, but the same phenomenon can be found there also. In comparing the two sites, 612 photos of babies or toddlers on their own appear in The Glades compared to 315 in El Mirador (Appendix Figure 1). In The Glades there are 415 images of the woman alone, posted by 23 women, whereas in El Mirador 1,006 images of the woman on her own were posted by 25 women. In The Glades there are usually also some images that ensure that the strong bonding between mother and infant has been captured and posted in its own right (Figs 6.34 and 6.35).

All of this is entirely consistent with studies conducted previously by Miller on practices of consumption and how they reflect the degree to which the birth of a baby is also the birth of a new person – a mother.[3] That is to say, in becoming a mother a woman is now someone defined by a relationship rather than existing in their own right, hence the title of Miller's earlier publication 'How Infants grow Mothers in North London'. Mothers can entirely replace themselves with an idealised version of their infant – partly because, just as with dogs and cats, the infant has no independent agency at this stage so anything can be projected on to them.

This profile picture album shows how quickly a mother can erase herself in favour or her infant

There are usually at least some images suggesting a strong mother–infant bond

Such self-effacement has to be seen in context, however, since it is by no means an isolated instance. In comparing the photos of individuals in England and Trinidad, a whole series of ways emerge in which the people of The Glades seem essentially indifferent to how they appear. It is not merely that they do not try to be glamorous or that, while we have many instances of 'bling' within Trinidad, this is entirely absent in The Glades. More importantly, it really doesn't seem to matter much at all what people are wearing when a photo is taken nor – more significantly – when they choose a photo to be posted on their own timeline (Figs 6.36, 6.37, 6.38 and 6.39). Typical images show men are wearing a T-shirt and jeans, while women may wear a dress or perhaps a shirt, but neither appear to have paid a lot of attention in choosing what to wear. Most of these women spend a reasonable amount of money both on clothes and appearance, for example when they go to work. Yet their Facebook pictures have an emphasis on looking causal and removed from the pressures of fashion. There is certainly no sense that they changed clothes for this photograph, nor that concern with what they were wearing impacted on the decision of whether or not to post the image. Clothes are decent and comfortable; they are simply not special. By comparison, these are core concerns within El Mirador. Appendix Figure 1 shows a total of 142 photos in The Glades where people seem to be drawing attention to what they are wearing, but these are mostly teenagers. In contrast, there are 576 in El Mirador. In a contrast even more extreme, we have only three instances in The Glades where a woman seems to be posing as a kind of faux model, compared to 142 such images from El Mirador.

There is a marked lack of concern
with what people are wearing,
at least compared to El Mirador

The contrast is just as striking when we move from clothing to the body. Trinidadians are very conscious indeed about almost every part and aspect of their bodies as these appear online, making the ways in which these are effaced in The Glades quite remarkable. As noted, the main problem with the 'no make-up selfie' was that so many of these women routinely went without make-up, as they explained to Miller and Ciara Green, and so could do nothing special for that photograph. They certainly care for their hair and nails, but again it didn't seem that they paid more than a few seconds of token attention to these matters when it comes to the images posted on Facebook.

Sometimes this effacement is quite extreme. We have cases of female graduates in their twenties, women who would generally be regarded as very good looking. But if one had wanted to show to another person that this was the case, it is simply not possible from the albums of photographs on their Facebook. There are simply no clear images of them at all, either in their own posting or as tagged, that can be used to demonstrate that they are good looking, let alone glamorous or sexy. The women may appear in the shade or background, but they have systematically avoided any such images. We found a few instances of this behaviour even among school pupils, but those were exceptional. As women grow older, this becomes more common. They are present within the material, but it is as though they have made an effort to avoid precisely the kinds of images that – not only in Trinidad, but in most countries of the world – would have been the key to the project of representing oneself on Facebook. They are there, but the image is not about them.

As an example, there are very few English photos in which it seems that legs are intended to feature as more than the part of the body which by default also appears in long-distance shots. The legs are included only because of the type of photo taken. They are not showing off their legs or using them as expressive of sexuality in the way that Trinidadians routinely would. There is a sense in which the body is essentially a 'nondescript', taking that word literally. It is effaced to the degree that there should be nothing at all that can be said about it.

If one looks at the images from holidays as discussed in Chapter 4, sometimes people appear in holiday shots wearing a bikini or swimming trunks. Even here, however, the photo is of them in the water smiling, or as foreground giving scale to the landscape and scenic elements. There are no images similar to those of the selfie girls, which represent a teenage phenomenon, or the Trinidadian exploitation of the beach precisely in order to expose and celebrate the body. Consistent with this is the degree to which the informality of these shots derives from women being photographed incidentally to what they are doing. A common shot that allows a woman to appear in the photo is as the person holding a baby. These may be more posed, with the woman smiling, but at other times she seems more like the prop enabling us to gain a better picture of the baby in question. One exception is when people dress up in fancy dress for a party, but this seems again to be typically English in that they are only allowed to feature as themselves while being made fun of. Some of these photos appeared in Chapter 4 (Figs 4.69, 4.70 and 4.71).

Of course as with all these statements, the term English or even 'The Glades' is an over-generalisation. We have seen that these claims would neither be true of schoolchildren nor of some of those who live in social housing. There are bound too to be some photographs, and indeed some people, that do everything our generalisation claims does not happen. These are generalities of social science, not natural science. They are precisely what we see 'in general', so an aberrant instance does not refute these arguments, as long as it remains uncommon. This is also one of those areas where a claim to quantification can easily become a kind of fake objectivity. We examined ten profiles of women aged around 30 or over. We found that out of 3,987 pictures there were only 191 that consist of pictures of that woman on her own, which reinforces this argument for self-effacement. It is more difficult when we come to more qualitative assessments. In our opinion out of nearly 4,000 photos there were only 15 (apart from wedding pictures) that seem posed so as clearly to display the item of clothing that a woman is wearing. This type of photo might elicit the comment 'I recognise that dress now, it's the one you bought in sunny Folkestone', or show someone dressed up to go out (Fig. 6.40).

Clearly the judgements behind such figures are subjective, but this may be balanced by the sheer scale of this evidence for lack of conspicuous display. What makes this most effective as an anthropological argument is that we are not focusing on any single feature. It is the combination of all of these observations around the effacement of the body, of clothing and the replacement of mothers by their infants, and the fact that men are even less likely to show concern with clothing and appearance, which when examined together suggest a general tendency towards modesty and keeping the individual from becoming the project of cultivation. A more general ethnographic treatment, which provides far more extensive coverage of modesty and self-effacement as a characteristically English trait, is found in Kate Fox's book *Watching the English*.[4]

6.40

Women posing to show off their clothing, as here, are remarkably rare in The Glades

Humour

Self-effacement is one of two ways in which people in The Glades distance themselves from being taken seriously or from becoming the centre of attention. Perhaps the still more English mode of retaining the centre ground and refusing to be drawn out is the use of humour. English humour is curious in various regards, but the most important quality from the perspective of this book's argument is humour being used not so much for being funny as for ensuring that nothing is taken too seriously. On Facebook, humour tends to organise itself around various genres. There are many, but here we will just briefly examine what seem to be among the three most common: the ability to project on to one's pets, the use of puns and the use of the word 'fuck'.

Funny cats

As noted above, the cat is well primed to express something analogous to the 'semi-detached' house. More than with dogs, the cat seems to possess an inevitable autonomy. It can therefore be a cuddled infant as well as a creature whose position of distance or disdain provides a humorous and critical running commentary on this same domesticity, of which it is the only half-acquiescing victim. One woman has got this potential down to a fine art with her long stream of funny captions; only a few are shown here to give a sense of what she uses her cat to do.

We can start with the integration of the cat into that most English of comic genres, 'toilet humour'. The following two images have the captions 'It's hard to concentrate on doing a wee with this staring up at you' and 'He's obsessed with the toilet. It's a nightmare when you need a piss' (Figs 6.41 and 6.42).

Cats can be good subjects for aspects of toilet humour

Generally cats have a far more positive image in The Glades than in El Mirador, often as here posed to look interesting or intelligent

Other typical posts that express this English sort of critical distancing would include the caption 'so judgemental' (Fig. 6.43).

The contrast with Trinidadian posting is that although cats may also be used there for humour, the tendency is either to make sexualised references (including the ambiguity of the term 'pussy') or to represent something more wild or even evil. In The Glades the genre of humour is much more respectful (Figs 6.44 and 6.45). In the latter image, the last line of the poster reads: 'He's not lost or anything. Just thought you should see him.'

Puns

Puns and plays with words are perhaps the bedrock of English humour. There are countless memes featuring wordplay, although people also just pun in text without resorting to visual memes (Figs 6.46, 6.47, 6.48 and 6.49).

There are also many memes that are a parody or give a twist to a theme. The 'Keep Calm' series is especially common. Also frequently used are images that play on ordinary life, or that make moral points through joking (Figs 6.50 and 6.51).

Sometimes cats command considerable respect

The pun remains the stalwart of English humour. It appears on Facebook in text and as visual memes

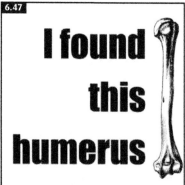

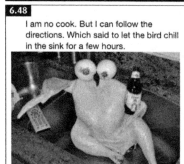

Second to the pun in English humour is irony or subversion, both also a feature of many posts

'Fuck' is funny

The other remarkably common form of humour is pretty much anything with the word 'fuck' in it, as in this series. Much more rarely, other words such as 'cunt' may work for particular instances (Figs 6.52, 6.53, 6.54, 6.55, 6.56 and 6.57).

'Fuck' stands out as funny in its own right, with much more occasional use of other swear words

There are many reasons why the word 'fuck' has this prominent role, but clearly one of them is that the word is used as a kind of check on what otherwise would be a trajectory towards taking something seriously. Often it seems that one was just about to take something as significant and worthwhile in its own right, whether doing the housework, religion or caring about other people. Just about to – but then, at the last moment, the word 'fuck' conveniently appears and saves you from this fate. Suddenly you realise that actually you 'don't give a fuck'. So the word may be used to deflate the self-regard of others, or the idea that we are supposed really to care about them. But equally it is used to prevent any serious self-regard or taking ourselves or our convictions too seriously. 'Oh fuck it' brings us back to what is portrayed here as the natural self, just in time.

If humour is to be employed to prevent any slippage into the seriousness of the moralistic and religious on the one hand, or the sexual and the libertarian on the other, then it helps if it is allowed to attack attempts to claim moral order directly. An obvious example would be religious images. Because of the specific nature of English liberalism, we do not find humour used against Muslims, Jews or any other target group where it might be seen as racist. Yet in The Glades images that Christians might find offensive do appear as posts (Figs 6.58, 6.59 and 6.60).

Posts from The Glades appear to indicate it is acceptable to make jokes about Christianity as the established religion of the state, but not other religions.

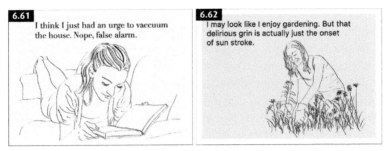

6.61 I think I just had an urge to vaccuum the house. Nope, false alarm.

6.62 I may look like I enjoy gardening. But that delirious grin is actually just the onset of sun stroke.

As noted in chapter 4, humour is often an antidote to the pressure of domestic tasks

If the desire is to avoid taking anything too seriously by returning to the middle ground, then a final logical problem presents itself. What if we also take the project of the suburban middle ground itself too seriously? It seems that the people of The Glades also need to ensure that being suburban and domestic is not seen as too serious an aim of life. On the whole, women seem to be delegated the craft and labour of the home, with men mainly involved in the manual side of DIY. So women have whole genres of humour devoted to not being seen as too serious about being 'domestic goddesses'. Here we find various jokes about housework and the home (Figs 6.61 and 6.62).

These may be taken alongside a series of images shown in Chapter 4, which focused on the role of wine. As noted, wine itself was not taken seriously as a subject, with such postings ensuring that they would not be seen as connoisseurs, or even French or Italian. Instead the simple generic 'wine' could be used to similar effect as the word 'fuck'. In those Facebook postings also the attitude seems to be about debunking potentially serious topics: 'Sod all that, let's just have a glass of wine.'

Serious posting

Most genres of serious posting are less common in The Glades than in El Mirador, but this chapter would considerably mislead if these were ignored entirely. For some of our English informants all Facebook is serious. This includes a few individuals whose strong religious beliefs dominate their postings, most of whom, but not all, are also elderly (Figs 6.63 and 6.64). The straw crosses pictured below were made by the person who posted them for Palm Sunday (Fig. 6.65).

Serious religious posting is much less common in The Glades than in El Mirador

Postings about religions other than Christianity, such as this one celebrating Ramadan, are relatively rare in The Glades

Some post religious activities within the village, such as crosses made for Palm Sunday

A single Muslim informant provided the only example of religious posting other than Christians (Fig. 6.66).

An exception to the infrequency of posting on serious topics seems to be references to current news. It seems acceptable to be serious in support of environmental/climate change/green issues, for instance, and there are postings on those themes. Yet serious political commentary was less common in The Glades than in El Mirador, suggesting again that many English people feel that it is precisely regarding serious issues that it is best to present one's posting in humorous terms. These would appear to be less true of postings from people living in social housing (Figs 6.67 and 6.68).

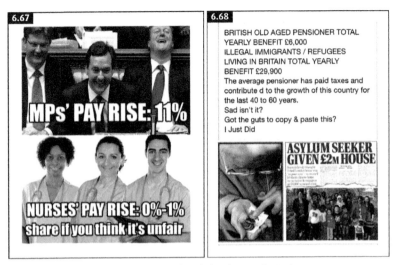

Political posting is also less common in The Glades than in El Mirador

In addition, some postings relate to the memory of those who were killed in the two World Wars, reinforcing our observation that the centenary memorial day for the First World War in 2014 was one of the best attended events during field work on The Glades. The two villages comprising The Glades lost 175 soldiers during the two World Wars (Figs 6.69 and 6.70).

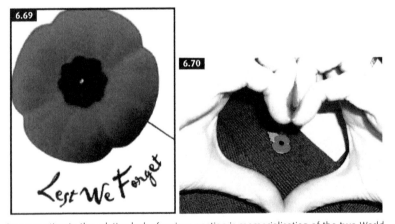

One exception to the relative lack of serious posting is memorialisation of the two World Wars, which remains a significant village event

Self-deprecation

While the last section acknowledges the presence of some genres of more serious posting, we have now discovered that, more generally, there are two legs upon which the English figure is able to stand: one is self-effacement and modesty and the other is humour. Given this, it seems entirely reasonable that the climax of this craft would have to be the combination of these two elements in what may be taken as the quintessential form of English humour – self-deprecation. Making jokes at one's own expense, for instance by wearing over-the-top Xmas glasses, seems to be the single most English mode of self-expression (Fig. 6.71).

Perhaps the most characteristic form of humour is self-deprecation, for instance in wearing deliberately ridiculous spectacles

For example, one sequence of images is taken by someone who clearly is trying to make fun of herself in pretty much every posting she makes. She dresses to look silly in a mock historical costume or pulls strange faces for the camera (Figs 6.72, 6.73 and 6.74). She also uses a snail as her profile photo. It may be no coincidence that she is also a generous individual who helps in village activities in various ways and is particularly good at embodying and expressing village values. Self-effacement is of itself a generous act, in which one suppresses the cultivation of the self in order to give entertainment to

This individual finds every opportunity to express this self-deprecating humour in her posts

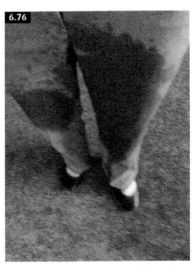

Mistakes are a frequent source of humour directed at oneself. 'Even I might have figured out that something wasn't quite right here !!'

English humour allows the possibility of almost revelling in a series of unfortunate events and of treating their embarrassing consequences with resigned self-mockery: 'Just not my day.'

others. She is by no means alone. Both males and females will find ways of using both text and images to achieve this form of humour.

Sometimes it is not a picture of the self, but rather a stupid thing that that person has done (and that now everyone else needs to know about) which provides the inspiration for the image, such as putting a plug socket in upside-down (Fig. 6.75) or suffering an unprofessional series of events: 'Spray myself when testing the shower, then shout 'shit fucker' in front of a potential tenant, now off to meet a landlord while looking like I've wet myself. Just not my day' (Fig. 6.76).

In one example a woman, rather than posting photos showing off her shoes, presents her swollen feet with the caption: 'Excuse the awful feet, but def know it's warming up due to swelling to my left foot...Every year it happens. No nice shoes for me...' (Fig. 6.77).

In another a woman posts an illustration of her own distracted behaviour with a caption of self-deprecating humour: 'Guess who was in a hurry this morning – How Embarrassing!' (Fig. 6.78).

As always images of children may contribute to the amusement, as in Fig. 6.79: 'Potty practice!!!! We have a long way to go I think!!'

As we shall see in the next chapter, people in Trinidad feel the need to confirm their glamorous and expressive selves at precisely the

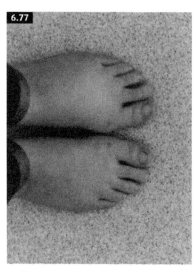

The embarrassing discovery that one is wearing non-matching boots is celebrated with a typical self-deprecating amusement: 'How embarrassing.'

In this post a woman shares an image of her swollen left foot with apologies for its appearance: 'Excuse my awful feet.'

same time that the English seek to disparage themselves. Self-deprecation may in some cases become effective self-effacement when subjects literally disappear from being their own profile pictures. This goes along with the elimination of the body as expressive and the general absence of explicitly sexual posts. In comparing this chapter with the previous two focusing on the English field site, we can see that the contrast is not only in relation to Trinidad, but also within the nature of Englishness itself. Of course some groups do not conform to these generalisations, for instance the posts of young people still at school, a gay male and some of those who live in social housing. But in a sense, precisely because these groups may feel excluded from the mainstream, their different posts in effect reinforce a dominant central ground that has no desire to be associated with any of them.

Posts of young children often provide scope for ironic humour, as in this image of a child playing in the bathroom: 'Potty practice!'

Two books provide the background to these English values. In her book *Watching the English*[5] Kate Fox examines the everyday behaviour of English people in a similar 'home counties' region. She is particularly successful at conveying the centrality of humour such as self-deprecation as well as the avoidance of extremes, based in a general modesty of self-expression which tries to avoid drawing attention to oneself. In many ways this chapter provides evidence that English people present themselves through visual media in ways that confirm her observations of conversation and everyday behaviour.

The most focused account of the wider context for this chapter is, not surprisingly, Miller's own volume on *Social Media in an English Village,*[6] since this is an account of the very same field site. This provides other grounds for English reticence based on a constant concern to protect the privacy of the domestic arena that has strong historical roots in English society. An inherent desire for privacy is directly threatened by the specific nature of social media as a mode that spans the traditional dualism of private and public domains. The people of The Glades were quite open about the threat that they felt social media posed to their traditional way of life, in which a net curtain preserved the sanctity of the private home combined with a limited gaze on to the public street. The primary argument of *Social Media in an English Village* is that English people re-purpose social media such as Facebook to create what Miller calls a 'Goldilocks strategy' of keeping other people at an appropriate distance: a clearly defined middle ground that avoids relationships becoming too hot or too cold. What this chapter adds to that argument is the evidence of how visual display corresponds to these concerns – by a combination of being circumspect and modest in the way one presents oneself online alongside the recourse to humour as the best response to any social threat or embarrassment.

7
Trinidadian cosmology and values

In this chapter we look at how postings on social media help us to understand the wider values expressed by and through Trinidadian society. One of the questions we posed when starting this project was whether an examination of visual posts, such as photos and memes, could provide the sort of insights into a society that one would gain from a more conventional ethnography. As it happens Miller had previously carried out just such an ethnography, published as the book *Modernity: An Ethnographic Approach*.[1] In that book he argued that it was possible to discern core values within Trinidadian society which took the form of a dualistic logic that expressed certain contradictions of modernity. He called these two sets of values 'transience' and 'transcendence'.

Transience encapsulates the values of the present, of immediacy and the life of the street. Partly as the result of a history of slavery and indentured labour, Trinidadians put considerable emphasis upon values that express their sense of freedom. Rather than a person being defined through longer-term institutionalisation, or being placed within a hierarchy, people want to be judged by that which they create for themselves, including their own appearance. This can also take the form of strong, overt (and sometimes explicit) sexuality, a sense of performance and bravado that used to be called 'boldface' and an identity that is judged by appearance. This is a world centred upon the street and reputation; since it is not institutionalised it must be attested to by others, for which social media provides the ideal platform. These values are brought to the fore by the festival of Carnival.

By contrast, Miller argues, the same ruptures of slavery and indentured labour led people to construct the values of transcendence, which focus upon creating long-term family projects involving creating roots and a sense of tradition. This ethos is characterised by education, religion, morality and domesticity. The values of transcendence are most fully expressed in the festival of Christmas, where the home and family are the key sites of celebration – even for non-Christian Trinidadians.

So slavery and indentured labour led to the development of these two contrasting constellations of value, manifesting the desire for freedom on the one hand and for roots on the other. This development of two antithetical poles is in stark contrast to The Glades, where society has been shaped by a very different history of gradual change over centuries. As shown in Chapter 6, the emphasis in The Glades is upon the middle ground as expressed in the values of the suburban compromise, by not wanting to stand out and by avoiding extremes.

Visibility and the visual

While social media generally leads to an increased emphasis upon visual communication, it has quite different ramifications in these two field sites. In Trinidad there was already an emphasis upon appearance as something that people cultivate. Since appearance is the result of a person's own actions it is seen as the 'truth' about who they are – and being on the surface, rather than being hidden, it is open to inspection by other people. By contrast, for people in The Glades, as reflected in the history of European thought, the surface is often derided as the merely superficial.[2] For adults, the truth of a person is felt to be deep inside them. On the outside we see a less authentic self: the surface is shallow, superficial and not to be depended upon. These notions of the self seem to stem from a society that was traditionally hierarchical and institutionalised; a person's 'truth' was assured by their blood or background.[3] For Trinidadians, by contrast, what was deep inside was hidden from view and therefore probably a lie.[4]

If people are defined more by appearance in Trinidad, then the visual postings found on Facebook might be expected to be seen as a closer reflection of who a person really is and so to have a greater resonance. We have argued along similar lines in previous publications such as *Tales From Facebook* and *Webcam*.[5] People in El Mirador do generally post more images. Appendix Figure 1 shows an average of 732 per person, as compared to an average of 450 images each in The Glades. However, as argued in these previous books, there are many complex elements to this concern with visibility.

In Trinidad Facebook is not only a space for visibility. It becomes a space for the expression of the two opposed forms of values termed transience and transcendence – both of which can take this potential for visibility to much greater lengths than we would expect in the kind of compromised middle ground favoured in The Glades. In this chapter we shall see many examples of this possibility, for instance when ordinary adornment and consumption develops into the more extreme forms of 'bling' culture, or when representations concerned with morality and sexuality extend to images that are clearly intended to shock and outrage and that cannot be ignored. Visual spectacle also has a long history in Trinidadian bio-politics, where the body is used as a site of resistance in social and political movements, riots and protests.[6] Carnival is the most obvious example, as the festival born out of a spirit of resistance by enslaved Africans and enacted by the body through performance.

Carnival and the values of transience

Fortunately this rather abstract argument is given very concrete form in Trinidad through the two dominant festivals of Christmas and Carnival. Even more conveniently, there is an obvious transitional moment during New Year's Eve, locally called Old Year's Night. This starts out as the most important church service of the year as the closure to the Christmas period, but the night ends in one of the most important parties of the year, the start of the Carnival period.[7] For the next six to eight weeks leading up to Carnival Monday and Tuesday, public life is dominated by a whole series of pre-Carnival parties called fetes.

Women tend to dominate Carnival itself and are much more likely to 'play mas' (play masquerade, or parade) in costume. Both men and women go to the pre-Carnival fetes, however – usually outdoor parties held all over the country. These vary from expensive, all-inclusive fetes which attract more elite groups to other 'bring your own drinks in a cooler' fetes which are open to anyone.

Fetes are mainly advertised and their tickets sold through the event pages on Facebook, where the organising committee give out their phone numbers to be contacted for buying tickets. Having purchased such tickets, people often show them on their timeline (Figs 7.1 and 7.2).

A good deal of time and attention is invested in the outfits people wear for fetes, and there are a lot of 'pre-going out' photos posted on Facebook (Figs 7.3 and 7.4).

Yet when people are at fetes, they prefer to be spotted and have photos taken of them by others. This has led to the rise of businesses based on photographing people at fetes specifically to post on their social photography website and on Facebook, enabling people to tag themselves

Tickets to fetes leading up to Carnival are exciting purchases and are often posted for others to admire

'Pre-going out' photos of outfits worn to Carnival fetes are frequently posted on Facebook for comment and display

or their friends (Figs 7.5, 7.6, 7.7 and 7.8). This represents an updated and more democratic version of traditional society pages in newspapers or magazines, but these social media photo businesses can be hired for any event by promoters or event organisers.[8] Such companies are hired

Social media photographers take photos of people attending fetes and share them on their business page on Facebook

for every large social event, with smaller businesses or individuals being hired for local bar events. So when young people go to fetes and events, they can expect to be photographed. In a society where appearance and visibility is so important, this also ensures the images that are circulated are from those occasions when they have spent most attention to style and clothing. But equally important is the public space itself: where one is seen, not just what one is seen in.

Even more expensive are costumes that are purchased for wearing on Carnival Tuesday. Masquerade bands mostly advertise their

Carnival masquerade bands have high-quality business pages on Facebook which advertise costumes

costumes through their band website and Facebook pages. Whether young women play mas (parade) themselves or not, many Trinidadians on Facebook 'like' these pages in order to look at costumes. The bigger bands have high quality professional photographs with professional models (Fig. 7.9).

El Mirador has its own mas camp[9] and carnival band with its own Facebook page to advertise costumes. Those created by the El Mirador mas camp are bold and dramatic (Figs 7.10 and 7.11). In this case the models for costumes are usually friends of the designers, or people who have themselves helped with making the costumes; they also share their modelling photos on their own pages.

The masqueraders subsequently post their own range of much less formal photographs showing themselves wearing the costumes on Carnival Monday and Tuesday; the photos are taken by other people who played mas with the band (Figs 7.12, 7.13 and 7.14).

People post fewer photos of actually playing mas (parading) because at that point they just want to concentrate on having a good time. So more photos are taken while they wait in the parade or snatch a quick break earlier in the day (Figs 7.15 and 7.16). Carnival photos are

Examples of the vivid and colourful costumes made by the masquerade camp in El Mirador

Informal photos, taken during Carnival Monday and Tuesday, show costumed participants dancing and celebrating on the streets

more of people posed and smiling than they are of dancing and partying; the latter appear more in images of the pre-Carnival fetes.

The lead up to Carnival also includes competitions for Junior Queens similar to beauty pageants for teenagers. Carnival is in fact just the tip of an iceberg of events and pageants in which people become

Posing and smiling for Carnival photographs helps to pass the time while waiting in the parade or taking a break

used to creating images that are glamorous, styled and posed (Figs 7.17 and 7.18). This lies behind the phenomenon of the 'faux model' shot discussed in Chapter 3 which resonates throughout the year and is far more common here than in The Glades.

The dance style seen as iconic of the Carnival season is 'wining': typically a man standing behind a woman, gyrating their hips together, though it is also entirely acceptable for women to wine on other women, especially as they far outnumber men at Carnival. At fetes the dance is more performative and provocative, including poses that mimic sex. There is an etiquette around photographing friends 'getting on bad' or showing their 'worst behaviour' – activities that mark what should happen for a fete to be deemed a success. At other times of the year, such photos wouldn't be taken and displayed. Yet Carnival is intentionally transgressive – here it is not only encouraged to 'free up' or 'play oneself', but it's also acceptable to take these kinds of photos and display them (Figs 7.19 and 7.20).

Nevertheless, friends may still be mostly discreet when taking photos of wining. Photos often only reveal the backs of heads or behinds and, unless people are in full masquerade costumes, we do not see many faces clearly. As a transgressive festival, Carnival can be a time when people can dispense with hierarchies and formalities. You can post photos of your boss wining and 'getting on bad', for example, showing that

In Junior Queens events, similar to beauty pageants, teenage girls learn to style themselves and pose

Only during Carnival are photos of 'freeing up' or 'playing oneself' taken and displayed

they too are capable of letting their hair down and getting into the spirit of Carnival fetes.

Carnival is the festival that most explicitly foregrounds transience, but the term refers to a far wider set of values found throughout the year. As a result, visual posts from Trinidad show more emphasis generally on glamour and sexuality than would be found in The Glades, and also the appropriation of style associated with forms of street culture such as hip-hop or gangsta aesthetics. Although Carnival is considered the time of year to 'play yourself', the idea that it is through the construction of the external self that a person reveals the truth about who they are is consistent.

As a result, the Facebook profiles of adults in El Mirador include more images of people going out for the night at any time of the year. Taking photos with friends in different venues, for example posed together in front of a bar or at a club, emphasises both looks and sociality (Figs 7.21, 7.22 and 7.23).

The Trinidadian term 'liming' is used in a similar way to 'hanging out' in other countries, but in Trinidad it is considered the core to social life. For the previous generation, liming would be more of a male activity, belonging to the world of the street: men limed in rum shops, discussed politics or other issues in a highly performative way and talked to, or about, the women who passed by. Today men and women lime together or in single-sex groups, but it retains certain key characteristics. Liming may start at one person's house, then without any fixed plan gather in others, or move on to a bar or club. At a weekend a group might get together and go to a beach or river, where people would cook or bring food. Drinking is considered central to most liming, but people also enjoy it for the sake of being together and enjoying sociality in a relaxed fashion, ideally with no time constraints.

At non-Carnival times of the year, styling oneself and going out with friends are still important

It is this sense of spontaneity and of not knowing what might happen next that brings out the element of freedom associated with transience. People then post images which try to capture something of these values. Typically such photos show people having fun or drinking, but they also pay some attention to how stylish their outfits are and how good they look (Figs 7.24, 7.25, 7.26 and 7.27).

As with Carnival, the orientation is to reclaiming the street and public space, putting oneself and one's body on show with no restriction of movement or behaviour. The modes of talk appropriate to the lime, banter and wit, are again highly performative, accentuating this ideal of putting oneself out for public display and validation. For all these reasons, posting images on Facebook feels like a natural extension of these prior modes of performative visibility (Figs 7.28, 7.29 and 7.30).

The logic of transience around performance and drawing attention to oneself extends to eye-catching accessories, such as elaborate nails for women or watches and jewellery for men. There comes a point at which these develop forms which are spectacular and difficult to ignore. This may be as true of the culture of appearance itself as the 'bling' phenomenon, replete with things that shine and sparkle: they are

Liming means going out and having a good time, ideally without time constraints.
In celebrating spontenaity and freedom, it is associated with the values of transience

Liming also includes celebrating physicality
and the body, and not restricting behaviour

worn precisely to draw attention. This aesthetic may also be extended, as we shall see, to visual postings that are extreme in their own right, featuring deliberately shocking, repulsive or sexually explicit content. Almost every aspect of this logic runs counter to that of The Glades, where almost as much effort may be expended in not standing out or drawing attention to oneself.

As such, 'bling' may be the result of careful, considered crafting of one's appearance. Make-up, hair and 'going out' nails all lend themselves to such styling (Figs 7.31, 7.32 and 7.33).

When nails are done at home, they might show one or two colours and some simple patterning. Those done in a salon, however, reveal their full potential as accessories, striking for their elaborate patterns and designs. Long, artificial nails are added, colours are bold and bright, and patterns can be extravagant with glitter, several colours and stick-on jewels (Fig. 7.34). Photos of nails are mostly close up, showing one hand either flat and horizontal or with the palm facing up and fingers curled inwards. The images are often posted by women who work in the salons themselves, if they are particularly proud of the day's creations, or by satisfied customers, who would then tag the nail technician or the salon. Similarly hairstyles are often posted after they have been especially done for a wedding or other occasion, as noted in Chapter 5.

Posting around 'bling' is especially common for men and women of lower-middle class and lower incomes, although the appropriation of

Like hair, nails are seen as the natural accessory of the body, to be styled and enhanced. The 'bling' ethos can extend to their highly elaborate, eye-catching designs

'bling' culture is also used by those who own businesses such as bars or work in fashion, where business is related to reputation and street culture. If women emphasise make-up and nails, the equivalent for men is 'metal' – especially gold, for which see the comments recorded in Chapter 8 (Figs 7.35, 7.36, 7.37, 7.38 and 7.39).

Sharing images of elaborate nail designs taken from other sources is also common

It seems that this bling aesthetic that pertains to the body finds new modes of expression when we explore how people draw attention to themselves through visual images posted on Facebook. For example, we find images clearly intended to be scandalous, horrific or overtly sexual – images that we felt could not be shown here. The content of these is in some ways resonant with another part of Carnival culture, that of *j'ouvert*, the opening masquer- ade, where people party in the middle of the night and into the sunrise of Carnival Monday morning. Historically people masqueraded in *j'ouvert* as creatures of the night, as devils or covered in mud, as well as figures

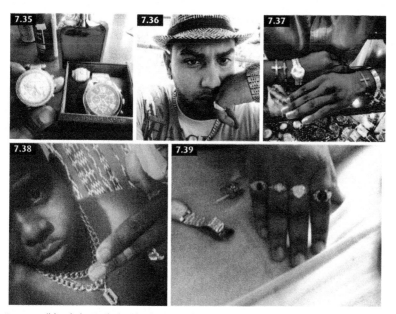

For men, 'bling' also includes displays of metal, in particular gold

relating to scandal and gossip about politicians, for example. The sunrise would expose these hidden things of the night, bringing them into the light of day. The logics of revelation and exposure are also in the vocabulary of *bacchanal*, the confusion which results from gossip and scandal. Trinidadians often seem to view bacchanal as the quintessential moment of Trinidadian culture.[10]

This tendency to reach out towards the extremes also applies to sexuality itself, where the more extreme and explicit images could be considered a sort of 'bling' sex. They are not common in El Mirador, but they are present, mostly posted by young men and discussed while sitting and drinking in bars. The idea of sex as a cause of 'bacchanal' may explain why we came across instances of what is now called 'revenge porn' in Trinidad, including a website dedicated to such images, some years before it was reported in the UK. Some Trinidadians were far more prepared to make the victim's identity clear when they publicly displayed sexual images from when they had been partners to these girls. Given the small size of Trinidad, this was more likely to lead to public humiliation and shame. Although mainly found on dedicated sites such as Triniporn, such images were also occasionally posted directly on to Facebook (Figs 7.40 and 7.41).

Sex photos were by no means the only genre that could be used to create shock or spectacle. During Sinanan's 15-month ethnography in El Mirador, there were at least three incidents where videos of schoolgirls

Extreme images of overt sexuality can also take forms such as 'revenge porn'

Other videos that cause shock and scandal include fights between schoolchildren

fighting went viral on Facebook. These were shared in the thousands, as were films of parents giving their children 'licks', a form of corporal punishment (Figs 7.42 and 7.43).

We are not suggesting that social media is the cause of such a phenomenon. Clear precedents can be found in the local newspaper industry, where images that attract a reaction of repulsion or disgust as a spectacle remain a common feature of their front pages and are clearly intended to cause outrage. For decades Trinidadians have been buying national newspapers with titles such as 'The Bomb', 'The Punch', 'The Heat' and so forth, which mix naked and semi-pornographic images of young Trinidadian women with images designed to titillate and shock taken from international media created for the same purpose, such as the US National Enquirer. Trinidadian news programmes and newspapers report violent crimes regularly, and the shares that are circulated on Facebook are often an extension of the sensationalism we see in the news, though they may sometimes be even more graphic in nature (Figs 7.44 and 7.45).

The values of transcendence

The study of visual Facebook posts here follows the logic of an earlier monograph by Miller, in which it was argued that these values of transience are created simultaneously with an entirely contrasting set of values expressing the concept of transcendence. Where transience finds its most explicit form in Carnival, the values of family, decency, education,

Sensationalism and graphic images also appear in mainstream news

religion and putting down roots associated with transcendence are celebrated through the festival of Christmas.

Christmas

Just as Carnival is much bigger than the event itself because a whole season of activities leads up to it, the same is true of Christmas in Trinidad. There are many postings on Facebook in the months leading up to Christmas concerning shopping, work parties and celebrations. The home is the focus of Christmas and the event involves a yearly ritual of cleaning and repainting, putting up new curtains and mounting an array of special Christmas decorations, including the tree. All of these may be the subject of Facebook postings (Figs 7.46 and 7.47).

Christmas is associated with both the family and the extended family as well as the wider community. At this time of year young people are also more likely to be more active in their communities, either by helping relatives, being involved in school events or undertaking more philanthropic work, for instance donating and contributing to Christmas hampers (Figs 7.48, 7.49 and 7.50).

Christmas is also a time that memorialises ancestors, and may supplement the anniversary of a death as a time to remember a loved one (Figs 7.51, 7.52 and 7.53). More generally, it is used to celebrate traditions.

Christmas in Trinidad celebrates family, tradition and establishing roots

Volunteering in the community or taking photos with family with Christmas decorations in homes or public spaces are fairly common

Christmas can also be a time to commemorate the passing of loved ones

Religion and nationalism

This is a period in which people make their religious beliefs explicit on Facebook, often through relevant memes. In Appendix Figure 1, seven out of 50 participants posted a total of 21 religious-themed posts in their 20 most recent posts, whereas only two people in The Glades posted religious images. Indeed, for some Trinidadians, religion is the dominant theme of posts on their Facebook timeline throughout the year. Trinidadians can be religious at all ages, but a common trajectory is to return to religious devotion around the time when one has a house of one's own and children (Figs 7.54, 7.55, 7.56 and 7.57).

Religious posting is found in relation to both Hinduism and Islam, although rarely as emphatic as with the Christian Evangelical churches who 'spread the word' through constantly posting images that they hope will inspire their followers (Figs 7.58, 7.59 and 7.60).

Trinidad is unusually ecumenical: everyone celebrates Christmas, Eid and Diwali. Indo-Trinidadians may post religious memes celebrating all three festivals. The 'likes' that religious posts and memes attract are more related to the sentiment of the post than the religion it belongs to, something people confirmed in discussion. However, sharing behaviour was different to 'liking', as people would only share posts and memes from their own religion.

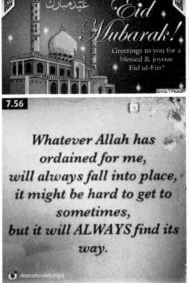

Religion is a dominant theme of Facebook posts throughout the year

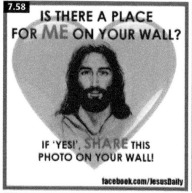

Evangelical Christians also post images
they hope will inspire others

Pentecostalism and Evangelism are associated with more didactic
religious posts, but these often use images taken from popular culture to
help make their point. There is something of an upsurge in the posting of
such images at the time of Carnival as a kind of 'warding off' of the evil
spirits associated with that festival (see Chapter 8).

More generally, however, people express the wider values of transcendence by linking both religious practice and ethnicity within a
general, family-oriented ethos, sharing photos of family or vocational
events (Figs 7.61, 7.62 and 7.63).

Serious informational posting and postings related to education
would come within this frame, though these seem less common than in
the English field site (Fig. 7.64).

By contrast, there is far more emphasis in Trinidad on nationalism, which is taken very seriously as ritual: all formal events are
preceded by standing for the national anthem. It is common to find
on Facebook memes associated with such nationalism, with a higher
instance around national holidays such as Emancipation Day or

Community, religious events and the family are expressive of the values of transcendence

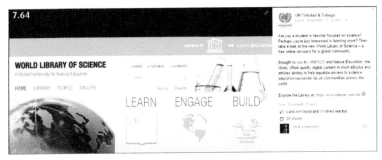

Informational and educational posts are less common than in The Glades, but they do appear

Independence Day. At international events such as conferences, club or sporting events, people may also express nationalism visually through décor and dress, for example wearing the national colours (Figs 7.65, 7.66, 7.67 and 7.68).

The values of transcendence seem to impact on the role of humour within El Mirador as compared to The Glades. Certainly banter, wit and other forms of humour are commonly used to diffuse situations, especially in small towns such as El Mirador, where families and friends have lived among their peers for decades and where grievances could have accumulated between people. They are also integral to transience, where they become performative and an aspect of visibility. But in The

Nationalism is expressed though décor and dress. It has a strong presence on Facebook, often through memes

Glades humour is found on Facebook commonly directed towards issues that might otherwise be seen as serious, including religion and nationalism. In Trinidad, by contrast, values associated with transcendence such as religion, nationalism and the family are seen as serious issues; they are much more rarely subject to humour. There is, however, also a notion of a specifically 'Trini' humour that people assume those from outside Trinidad would not 'get' (Figs 7.69 and 7.70).

Vocational interests

A key factor that helps transcendence coalesce into a consistent set of values in Trinidad that is again very different from The Glades is the treatment of work. This topic is central to Facebook in El Mirador and largely absent from Facebook in The Glades. One can see the continuity with posting on themes such as religion, in that for some the attitude to entrepreneurial activity seems to include an almost evangelical

'Trini' humour is also quite common, as in the memes which make fun of 'Trini' mothering ('mudda') and a parody of the 'Keep Calm' meme which asks: 'I'm a Trini, what the arse is calm?'

component, being promulgated as though it constitutes a life purpose (Fig. 7.71). There are no less than 20 places of religious and of entrepreneurial 'worship' in El Mirador, and each has its own dedicated following. Here we will examine two: a church named Faith Community and a network of Amway distributors.

Faith Community was established by a pastor and his wife who moved to the States to train as missionaries in the early 2000s and then returned to spread their message to the communities where they grew up. The congregation is less than five years old; it has a following of around 100, including several aged under 20 who are avid users of social media (Fig. 7.72).

Vocational projects are also invested with a sense of life purpose

A religious post from a member of Faith Community Church

The Pastor of the church was a strong advocate for using Facebook to spread the church's message. He would also post messages and blessings for Easter and Christmas and throughout the year, although he has also found Facebook somewhat distracting and intrusive, taking up his time in sifting through postings to find material relevant to the church and its ministry. Similarly his wife would post photos of church events around Christmas and games days, as well as family holidays. The couple experienced a negative backlash around this visibility of their family life, which became the subject of jealousy, and they have since deactivated their Facebook accounts.

However, members in the youth group have continued to post around their family, friends and beliefs to reinforce visibly the nature of community to the church. The youth ministry also post events such as church camps or sports days on Facebook and share Bible verses and religious or inspirational memes on their timelines.

Amway, 'American Way', is a US-based company that manufactures household items sold through personal networking or multi-level marketing rather than stores. Individuals buy their own franchise, but are given constant incentives by the company to build up a network of distributors to increase their own profit. This creates a hierarchy in which managing other people as distributors provides greater rewards than selling the goods oneself.

At an Amway meeting, the atmosphere resembles that of charismatic worship – full of high-energy call and response, played between speakers and intended to generate motivation and enthusiasm. Visibility is a major part of Amway's rhetoric, with an emphasis upon the display of professionalism and success. Higher ranking individuals need to 'look the part' in order to gain trust and authority, with men wearing suits and women wearing tailored skirts, blouses and jackets. Teams may wear the same colours.

Facebook is then considered an extension of the visibility afforded by meetings. For example, a very successful young couple post images that show them at conferences and events, speaking in public and meeting with other successful partners in the US. While the husband posts more motivational quotes and memes that focus on individual hard work and success, the young wife posts around their baby and family, emphasising their well-rounded family life (Figs 7.73, 7.74, 7.75 and 7.76).

Another woman posts motivational memes when she is stuck in traffic or comes home in the evening to show that she is always thinking about the people with whom she is working and encouraging them from afar (Fig. 7.77). She also uses her Facebook page to advertise some of the

Posts by a young couple of Amway Independent Business Owners, emphasising the company's ethos of combining business success with happy family life

"THE ONLY THING STANDING BETWEEN YOU AND YOUR GOAL IS THE BULLSHIT STORY YOU KEEP TELLING YOURSELF AS TO WHY YOU CAN'T ACHIEVE IT."
– Jordan Belfort

goods such as cosmetics, which fits into a genre of posting around make-up and style in Trinidad (Figs 7.78, 7.79 and 7.80).

The use of Facebook by such groups seems to extend the values enshrined in transcendence, just as bling and scandal extended the values associated with transience. Both the Amway and the Faith com-

A motivational meme posted by another Amway Independent Business Owner

munities take advantage of the visual platform of Facebook to create the feel of an imagined community, in Anderson's sense of a collective that individuals can identify themselves with as part of the group.[11] They attempt to fill in for what they feel the state has failed to provide and, through religion and entrepreneurship, give an alternate means for a group identity where one can achieve individual aspirations as well.

There are many other variants of this form of evangelical entrepreneurship. One we encountered in El Mirador Facebook postings was the sales meetings for an

Our Greatest Fear is Not that We Are Inadequate but that We Are Powerful Beyond Measure

Images of appearing successful, motivation and goods for sale are typical for Amway IBOs

expensive version of coffee called Organo Gold. These tended to attract low income people from squatting areas interested in becoming sales representatives, who otherwise might have exemplified the values of transience. As noted in these examples, the religious and entrepreneurial content is often blended with photos of happy, successful couples and memes with serious messages around hard work and perseverance – as well as an emphasis upon family, togetherness and setting down roots for the future.

While these examples represent aspirational motivations, often including people with less education, when we look to people with university degrees we see a greater concern to adopt strategies that are seen as more sophisticated. For example, the Rotaract group in El Mirador are in their twenties and early thirties, the youth wing of the traditional Rotary club found alongside similar philanthropic groups such as Lions and Kiwanis. They all have strong local ties, with local schooling or parents involved in local businesses. Their Facebook postings and shared memes would be closer to those found in The Glades, revealing an increasing emphasis upon more environmentally-conscious and green

Young people involved with the Rotaract club also emphasise environmental concerns, in posts that have similarities with those of The Glades

International messages of environmentalism are particularly resonant in relation to endangered Caribbean sea turtles

issues, both locally and in relation to global concerns such as climate change (Fig. 7.81). However, an effot is made to combine such international messages with more local Trinidadian idioms, such as showing concern for native species (Fig. 7.82).

These middle-class groups are particularly cosmopolitan. Young women look at international fashion blogs and YouTube videos, in many ways reflecting whatever causes such 'clean-cut' groups are espousing worldwide. These include the recent development of environmental and outreach work, ranging from beach clean ups to packing hampers to distribute to the poor at Christmas. They also emulate the crafts and baking associated with worldwide trends in the revival of knitting, crocheting and fabric work and cake decorating, and are entirely at one with people in The Glades in their current emphasis within this genre – which is, of course the cup cake (Figs 7.83 and 7.84).

It is important to note that for the Rotaractors, as for almost all Trinidadians, there is an expectation that they will associate themselves with elements of transience as well as transcendence. In addition to frequent photos of a group of them liming, their posts also show traits such as humour, dialect, poses, drinking and sociality, each with their specific Trinidadian inflection. They will espouse the better class of all-inclusive pre-Carnival fetes and hope that photos will then circulate on Facebook showing that they were present (Figs 7.85, 7.86, 7.87 and 7.88).

Other worldwide trends include cupcake decorating

Rotaractors are community-oriented, but also embrace liming and having a good time

This is in no way an anomaly. The key to understanding the content of this chapter is to realise that the core difference between El Mirador and The Glades is not just that people in El Mirador espouse the values of transience and transcendence rather than the middle ground of suburban England. It is rather that they espouse both of these *simultaneously*. Trinidadians want to be both local and global, to have fun and to be religious, and they want to show their affinity to these values at a personal as well as a group level.

Dualism and bacchanal

The emphasis in The Glades upon occupying a middle ground of compromise and moderation creates not just a homogeneity of postings, but also an internal consistency in the posts of a given individual. By contrast, in El Mirador, many people exhibit a clear dualism within their own Facebook postings. That is to say the same person may post not only staunchly Christian and moralising memes, but also images of explicit sexuality and scandal – often juxtaposed on the same timeline.

We will present one mild and one more extreme example. Fig. 7.89 shows a young man with his Rotaract peers winning awards and on a field trip, images that show community values. But we also see photos of liming, drinking and having fun, photos that the young man described as showing him 'as a real person' (Fig. 7.89).

In the second example we see a more extreme dualism. Here a young man continually posts memes side by side that represent both a strong religiosity and also explicit sexuality (Fig. 7.90). There were many examples of this kind of posting, among women as well as men.

While people do not find it a problem to juxtapose these apparently opposed values, they are entirely aware that visual images as a form of revelation can have consequences. They recognise that Facebook itself encourages a culture of nosiness and gossip that can lead to scandal and bacchanal. Facebook is often known as Macobook, referring to the local term 'to maco', which means prying into other people's business without their consent (Fig. 7.91). It is possible that Facebook has led to people being increasingly conscious and explicit about these effects. Terms such as 'real talk' and bacchanal certainly existed prior to Facebook, but the platform provides a new forum for their discussion and dissection. Bacchanal may emerge on Facebook through direct comments on images, for example the caption accompanying this posting which means 'Miss, I take your man for the entire Carnival week, he says he's hot for you, see how I'm wining on him, lol' (Fig. 7.92).

An example of posts of a young man in the Rotaract club that shows both serious and less serious aspects of his vocation

A more extreme example of dualism which shows strong religiosity and explicit sexuality

'Macobook', a Trinidadian nickname for Facebook, refers to the local term 'maco', meaning to look into another person's business unasked

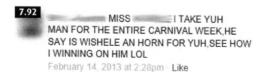

Bacchanal appears directly through posts intended to provoke and cause scandal

An emotionally charged update that does not directly refer to another person

Another genre of posts that can lead to bacchanal, but seems to be strongly associated with the rise of social media more generally, is the 'indirect'. Here an (often emotionally charged) update is posted, but without stating at whom the particular barbed comment is aimed. Examples of indirects from El Mirador include: 'The more they say, the more I pray' or 'Inactions speak louder than actions' – or the comment on honesty that accompanies this post (Fig. 7.93).

We also see Facebook postings which expose the pretentiousness that Trinidadians consider comes from being too serious about transcendent values. In mid-2014, for instance, a series of memes circulated featuring Kermit the Frog, based on an advertisement for Lipton tea. It portrays Kermit sitting watching chaotic New York City from the inside of a café, sipping calmly a cup of Lipton tea. The catchphrase for the meme, 'But that's none of my business', is used to highlight what another person or group is doing wrong (Figs 7.94 and 7.95). While also found in other societies where these memes circulate, this particular combination of humour, moralising and 'truth' is typical of Trinidadian cultural ideals of bacchanal. The memes are, in effect, also a comment on how Facebook itself, and the meme as a genre, can participate in these cultural practices.

Part of a popular series of Kermit memes that moralise and speak the 'truth' through humour – a combination characteristic of bacchanal

Conclusion

We started this chapter by asking whether through the analysis only of visual posts we could reach the same conclusions as a more 'traditional' offline ethnography, such as Miller's book *Modernity: an ethnographic approach* (1994). Of course that was somewhat disingenuous; we have written this chapter in full knowledge of this earlier work and have adopted its terminology for our analysis. But at the very least we can state that it has not been at all hard to analyse this visual material as expressive of the same dualism that was the subject of the earlier study; indeed we would like to think that this would have become evident through our current analysis of visual postings on Facebook even without this precedent. The key point of this volume is that values on social media only really become clear when we see how they contrast with those of another society. Thanks to the visuals posted on Facebook, we actually do 'see' these contrasts.

This chapter has affirmed the existence of two clear sets of values, which we have called transience and transcendence. Transience refers to the temporary, the egalitarian, the free, and the world of reputation and the street celebrated in the festival of Carnival. Transcendence describes the desire for roots and permanence, the values developed through continuity of home, family, work, religion and community and most fully expressed by the festival of Christmas.

That this dualism should migrate so easily and clearly to Facebook is hardly surprising when we consider the introduction to this chapter. Here we pointed out the importance of appearance, surfaces and visibility itself in Trinidadians' core idea of what constitutes the truth of personhood; for them this lies on the surface, subject to the judgement of others, and is not hidden away in their deep interior, the place of lies. Once again this is the exact opposite to the beliefs of people of The Glades, for whom the truth and substance of a person lies deep within; outside is the domain of superficiality and mere appearance, and is viewed as potentially deceptive. This is one of the reasons why adults in The Glades seem almost to stress how little attention they have paid to how they look when their images are posted online. For them there is a concern that Facebook might present a false or more superficial version of their true selves.

In stark contrast, if you ask a Trinidadian to summarise the essence of being Trini in one word, it is quite likely that the word will be bacchanal. As anthropologists, we need to respect and explain that choice.

It seems to follow quite naturally from the juxtaposition of these three facets of Trinidadian cosmology: the idea that the truth of a person lies on the surface, the drive towards visibility, and the set of values that coalesce around transience on the one hand and transcendence on the other. In a context in which visibility makes this juxtaposition obvious, there is a clear potential for subsequent scandal and confusion, which is what the term bacchanal celebrates. But the final point is that this is indeed celebrated rather than denied. It is felt that such visibility, in bringing the truth of a person into the public light, is itself a positive, exposing what might otherwise be falsehood and deception. This is why in *Tales from Facebook* it was clear that in some respects Facebook itself has come to be regarded as the book of Truth.[12]

8
Ten points of view

This chapter has a rather different intention than the others. So far we have written largely from the perspective of the anthropologist as analyst of social values at a level of abstraction which most people have no reason to consider. By contrast, this chapter presents the comments made by Trinidadians themselves. The reason was not because we think that our informants' opinions represent a more direct or authentic truth. Rather it is to show that there is considerable variety in the ways in which people interpret the same image. Indeed the same individual may consider an image to have several possible meanings, and be in some doubt as to which one to favour. These informants generally regarded the question as to why someone posted any particular image as a puzzle to be contemplated in much the same way that we did. They assume that people constantly change their minds, posting an image one day and the next saying to themselves 'What WAS I thinking?' When we use the word 'Trini' it is in recognition that there is a constant discourse within Trinidad as to what is typically Trinidadian. We do not use it to homogenise actual Trinidadians, who represent an extremely varied population.

There is, however, another, crucially important point to this exercise which will gradually emerge during this chapter. Everything in this book depends upon the ideas of the typical. In as much as people do conform and do create typicality, we need to investigate the mechanisms and pressures that may account for this. Perhaps the single biggest pressure is other people's responses to what we post. So this chapter explains the process of how cultural normativity is created and maintained, and that shows how the rest of the book is even possible.

We conducted this work in Trinidad, but not in The Glades, simply because Trinidadians enjoy openly discussing and criticising images while people in The Glades are much more circumspect and embarrassed by such a request. We carried out this exercise by showing images we had gathered from El Mirador to Trinidadians living in Port of Spain; they would not recognise the anonymised people concerned and so would feel free to comment based on the visual image alone. We showed 50 images to our 10 informants, but for reasons of space include only those that elicited the most extensive responses, and therefore best illustrate the points we want to make in this chapter.

The 50 postings we used were intended to reflect the range of people in El Mirador as described more fully in Sinanan's own book within the 'Why We Post' series.[1] The 10 people we showed these postings to consisted of six women and four men, most in their late teens or twenties, which is the dominant age group posting on Facebook in this site. They mainly came from a lower income area, but had better than average educational levels for people from that area. A factor that should be kept in mind is that because they all come from Port of Spain, the capital city, and knew that the postings were from some lower income region they would have regarded as 'country', the tone of these comments has something of the scorn of the town mouse looking down on the country mouse. No doubt if the exercise were reversed, the people of El Mirador would have been equally derogatory about the inauthentic, pretentious and 'stush' character of those postings. But what they have in common is a Trinidadian penchant and rich dialect of disparagement.

The first two posts we examined were helpful in gaining a sense of the importance of vocabulary for describing people (Figs 8.1 and 8.2). One of our informants called this individual 'a wet man',[2] which could mean 'a lot of girls, a lot of money, a lot of clothes, always in the latest brands, trends. So that seeing that you could show the girls: I'm a handsome guy, I could dress, I have a lil vest, I have a lil gold chain'. Another called him 'Dudes man, yeah he look like he now coming up,

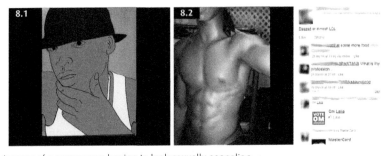

Images of a young man hoping to look sexually appealing

kind of thing. He now probably getting a lil – facial hair.... muscle and he want the girl to see, so prob have a few girls chatting him down. My sister would say "hot man" "wet man".' To a third, the image seems to say 'yeah I posing, gallerying, this is me. Yeah that's all he saying, this is me. Gangsta style, showing off his fedora, gold chain, just showing off to my friends'.

Another woman described him as a 'Tusty guy'. She explained 'well, the expression could be said like a dog who panting for water. So they use it for guys who running down women, like thirsty for women. So he saying there are so many "tusty" guys on Facebook. It's embarrassing me.' A fifth informant explained: 'This looking like one of those blingers, players, who just tryna glam before the camera, show off the look... somebody hip, stylish, usually with a lot of gold blinging as we see here, gold teeth, gold chain like a rapper. Tryna emulate the vibe of a rapper or a person who just out there, who live large, you know do things to the extreme. Decadent lifestyle... This looking like a man who tryna hook up with some girl out there.'

Another described him as 'swell-headed... a lot of people would put a picture like that, and you see them in Port of Spain the next day and is like a normal short pants, nothing'. Yet another responded by saying: 'they looking delinquent, and I would probably assume he going be one of those, you know those schools where you would stereotype the students as being bad. How he have his hands on his face, that's a kind of bad man or gangster kind of look. And then he also wearing the chain and the vest. So I don't know if the reason he might post that is to fit in with his peers. Maybe he have that kind of culture with him.' While this comment tries to narrow and pigeonhole the look, the next does the opposite: 'That's a typical Trini man, kinda "I real sexy boy!" kinda "look yuh know", and the fedora and the gold chain, yea that's what it is, typical, typical Trini man.' Finally one girl responded: 'Wow, I am speechless, I'm sorry. Well, why would somebody put that up? They too nasty. They so Trini that I have to laugh at them sometimes, but it's really a slack... this one is really slack, but I find it so.'

Another term that could be used of this image is 'metal', as in "I could go in work right now and one of the co-workers would say "Boy I went and lime last night, bounce in d' dance, real metal around my neck".' This obviously refers to the gold chain which one of our informants held as particularly significant 'because gold is a hit thing right now in the country. Gold is a lot of money and as the trend is now, gold could allow you to get a lot of things. Gold could allow you to get a lot of girls, that have a lot of money, plus you might get a lot of clothes.

The main thing is really the gold that he have around his neck.' [D: 'You still use words like bling?' I: 'Nah bling, don't really…']³

Three main points arise from these responses. The first is that most terms used are as much about making a judgement as a description, no doubt facilitated by the fact that these were not people they actually knew. Secondly, these informants are just as ready to engage with the question of typicality, based on the idea that there is a characteristic 'Trini culture', as any anthropologist. Thirdly, this is a place with an extraordinarily broad-ranging vocabulary. In the experience of both Miller and Sinanan, Trinidadians are typically extremely articulate and verbal compared to people in other places where we have lived. Skill in talk is highly valued, and although people here have far lower levels of education than The Glades, it is much harder to keep up with the sheer richness of expression in Trinidad, especially in the use of innuendo. Not that this is consistent. One person is happy to use the term 'bling', for instance, while the final informant avoids it.

Establishing morality

If description of these images is typically also judgemental, then it represents a system for establishing moral positions. We will explore this in three stages. Firstly, we consider how people establish their sense of morality and its boundaries. Secondly, we will look at how people 'put other people down'. Thirdly, we will see how the combination of these two creates the conditions for establishing normativity. The word *normative* is central to anthropology. This whole book is actually about normativity, as are most books in anthropology. Our premise is that individuals will always try to establish what the people around them regard as appropriate and inappropriate behaviour. These may not be enforceable. We may decide to act in a way other people dislike or disdain, but the point is that we are aware how others will judge us. So the present chapter helps us to understand previous chapters as cultural generalisations. Because most people most of the time prefer to avoid such disdain, the result is that most postings conform to what is 'approved'. In the next three posts, we see how the comments about images are used to make clear what the viewer sees as the boundaries that should determine what is or is not acceptable for a posting in Trinidad. The focus is on a genre where this policing of boundaries is particularly pronounced, that of sexualised images.

In the first, we see two girls posting a photo that shows them having a good time at a party (Fig. 8.3). They would probably have welcomed the first comment 'OH LORD I COMIN N STORMIN DAT DINNER', likely a friend who is tempted to come there uninvited ('stormin') to join them. Our informants noted what is displayed – their dresses, the weave in their hair, the fact that they are hot and 'wassy,' have good bottoms and are having fun. The pose is of them 'wining' – the dance form associated with Carnival where it is very common for one female to wine on the arse of another, especially as far more women than men dance in Carnival.

Two women enjoying themselves at a party

In response some felt this is exactly what they should be doing, having fun. But others say: 'It's nasty, they look like whores, especially the one at the back.' They are seen as promoting 'slackness'. For others, the issue is one of context. This would be acceptable within Carnival, but outside of that 'I not homophobic, but I know I don't want no woman wining on me.'

Informants saw the fact that the woman had posted this image as a deliberate attempt to show off her 'assets': 'Let's parade to the world. Let's parade my boobies to the world' (Fig. 8.4). Another suggests 'That one, to me she saying – boobies rule'. The photo is seen as reflecting the way Trini men focus mainly on 'tits and arse'. 'The person seems like they in love with her breast. Most likely, the husband who taking those photos and he's proud of what seeing.' 'If she posted a picture of her full self that would be fine. I think she's drawing attention to a certain area, and a lot of women they post these pictures and they would feed off of the comments.'

There is plenty here informants find to disparage. 'That's her bra underneath this? It's a sun dress. Look, I see strap things there. Eww, that's wrong.' Or they comment on her figure. 'Chunkalunks…you ever heard that word?' [D: What does it mean?] I: 'Is like a term that means kinda round, kinda thickish. Is like a discreet way of saying you're fat, chunky, chubby. Also is a term of endearment.'] There is also considerable speculation on what she is drinking and how much she has already drunk.

A woman showing off her physique

A woman posing in her carnival costume

The issue is more precise with the final example of a photo of a woman who has posed in her Carnival costume (Fig. 8.5). Usually this is seen as expected and appropriate. Given how much money people spend on their costumes, they would naturally want to post a picture of themselves looking good. This involves not only wearing the costume, but also the display of the body as fully inhabiting it. The local expression is that 'I playing mehself'. This can be explained as: 'Is like I not holdin back, no restrictions…play yuhself, break free, doh worry what anybody say, you just doing what you want, where you want, yuh know. You just doing thing without any kinda consideration. You ain't offending anybody or whatever. Is like a reckless abandon…an just the way she have that…I seeing like I playing mehself here. I come to get on bad. I come to get on wassy.' Similar lyrics are found in countless Carnival songs and this 'freeing up,' or going beyond the everyday, is precisely the point of Carnival.

So almost every element of this image is entirely acceptable. Almost – because one part of it is not accepted even within that Carnival context: 'Her breasts basically out and sure she could see the dark area around the nipple is showing and normal people wouldn't do that.' Another informant observed: 'I could almost imagine I think I'm seeing areola down in the corner there. That goes too far.' This is what we mean by policing the boundaries – determining the precise point at which things are no longer acceptable.

Putting people down

There are many ways boundaries can be established, with praise as well as insults. But this was a context in which our informants had nothing to lose by having fun at the expense of those who posted these images. So the emphasis was on being extreme and showing off through the type and degree of the put down. The trait that was most subject to this was any suggestion of pretension. The term 'sweet man' is already ambiguous in Trini dialect (Fig. 8.6). It still means sweet in the sense of 'caring' or 'attractive', but it also has connotations of 'sweet talk' – the way men use language to get women to do things they really don't want, or shouldn't want, to do.

The informants assumed that no man would construct such an image for himself, but that the woman who made it had done him no favours since it made him into a 'pimp with flowers, that is an automatic strike off from sweet man'. One suggested: 'This person tryna diss him or something because this cannot be her man!' Or even that this is in fact a man 'that

A 'sweet man'

has a vendetta or something against him and tryna make him look bad or something'. Worse still, the man is seen as quite old, but the style of the posting is that of a young girl, so this particular man should not be fooling around with a girl of this age. Others describe him as 'pathetic', also as a 'gyalis' (a girlist), that is, a man who tries to get a girl anywhere.

There is a rich repertoire of implied claims: 'a sweet man is like a heart breaker, I love to break hearts, I entitled to do it. Yeah a sweet man is the male jargon here. Is a good thing, is like, you know you – a king, a sweat man, you know all the moves to make, you know all the right things to say, you know how to win over the ladies. All the different ins and outs, the tricks of the trade. Just showing how hot he is. Thinking he could get a woman with gold chain around his neck and thing.' But she concludes, 'Those things don't impress me though'.

At first glance this seems an innocuous enough post, but the resulting comments show how what might be termed its underlying semiotic richness can be mined by a critical observer to pretty much tear it to shreds (Fig. 8.7). 'The shades, even though you can clearly tell it's dark out, he's got the shades on. The ultimate symbol of coolness, of youth and being cool. So he has the shades on and yuh know the haircut, so I think that's it.' Or 'In fact not actually drinking – just put it to his mouth to take the picture'. Somewhat more brutal was the comment: 'douche bag...he not even drinking. And first of all he's drinking Carib Pilsner which is less calories – like – come on – who you trying to fool, that have less alcohol. Then the big shades in the night.' Finally the fact that this is a selfie provided still more grounds for the assault. 'I would say that is kinda sad'....

A man hoping to look cool

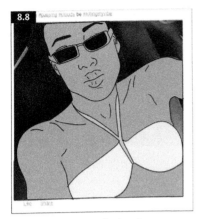

A woman relaxing at the beach

well maybe if the reason for him posting is to show that he is out doing something, but he himself took it. It's kind of... what's the word... kind of fake in a certain sense. Yeah, he's showing himself off as if he's out doing something – but then again he's by himself.' To summarise, the informants see a man trying to look cool by taking a selfie. But for them wearing shades at the wrong time, drinking a lower alcohol beer, or not even drinking it, and being on your own betrays another, rather less cool, side to this image.

Similar remarks are directed to the next image (Fig. 8.8). 'Her facial expression. Her glasses needed to be off. I take my glasses off for my selfies. Because you don't want glare. So the fact that she keeps her glasses on, she's not a person that usually takes selfies.' In a second case: 'Well she looking like she pouting there. It looking like a pout... the glare on the eyes there... I can't really tell what's the expression, well... it looking like she tryna advertise that she have thick lips, seductive lips that kinda thing... come and get me kinda thing.' [A third was asked by D: 'But you think she looks good in that?' I: 'No, I hate that face' D: 'Because?' I: 'It's fake.']

In the last three cases criticism is justified because the posting is viewed as pretentious or fake. But even without such justifications, people find things to condemn.

Most people saw the next image as rather 'sweet', testimony to the loving relationship of a couple (Fig. 8.9). They speculated whether they were married or siblings or a couple dating. Others criticised the clothes as not really suited to what should have been a party-like celebration. Most of all, they criticised the cake. As one put it: 'It could have been very last minute and they couldn't have gotten a cake. So they rush to Hi-Lo or Pricesmart to get one. They could buy that cheesecake in either of the places.'

Similarly with this next image, which would seem to be merely a rather benign attempt to give thanks to some good teachers and to the school (Fig. 8.10). Several informants found it quite amusing that teachers would be congratulated with a card containing the grammatical error of an inappropriate apostrophe. Others speculated that if this

A couple celebrating with cakes

Post giving thanks to a good teacher

had been made by the teachers, they must be very 'full of themselves' to have made such a self-congratulatory posting.

Picture of pet dog

Establishing normativity

If we now combine these two elements of establishing moral boundaries and putting people down, we can see how these become foundations for the larger project of establishing cultural normativity. The normative is by no means constrained to the arena of morality. Almost anything can be considered either appropriate or inappropriate.

This next posting would be entirely positive, and indeed common, were it from The Glades. But it is seen as entirely inappropriate for Trinidad (Fig. 8.11). In England pets are kept inside the house, but in Trinidad dogs are assumed to be always outdoors. Indeed this was seen as so strange that the issue was not used to condemn the owner so much as to infer that they couldn't be Trinidadian. 'Well yeah, that's definitely not here. Well not definitely, but chances are it might, is possibility it's not from Trinidad. If it is from Trinidad . . . it could be, but the common thing is put the dogs outside.' Similarly another person noted: 'Yeah, they not looking like they're from Trinidad. I don't think they're from Trinidad. But is always what kind of dog you have, and at the same time I know that in Trinidad, not much people is have their dog inside.'

From this develops a further logic: that if the owner is Trinidadian, they are trying to assert class distinctions by taking up this more

Fig. 8.12: Picture displaying cooking

international style. This seems reasonable on the basis that it is a very expensive breed of dog. 'Well, let's say in Westmoorings (a wealthy part of the capital) then. That's a high class area and sometimes some of the people that live there have quality dogs like that.' Or: 'When I see someone who has an animal that lives in the inside that's the stereotype that the person have money or middle class or probably white.' Indeed one informant makes clear that this is how she would like herself to be seen: 'Well it just normal, it just chilling on the couch. So if I could get a dog like that, I have no problem with a dog in the house.' Another disagreed: 'You know I kind of see animals as being dirty creatures. I guess it's because of, well, I never really used to take proper care of our dogs – so the idea of the dog being inside and being on the chair . . . ' Finally another informant mimicked what they saw as an old-style rural curse: 'What! Dog inside the house is ok? Get your tail outside and in the kennel. Lock you up and I will throw hot water on you and kill you later.'

Trinidadians are often fiercely egalitarian, with a rich culture of disdain for anyone who thinks they are better or superior. It is unlikely that most people would have come across the term focaccia, but would simply assume that it is pretentious cooking (Fig. 8.12).

The current term for describing pretentious behaviour is 'stush', with connotations a bit more derogatory than the English word 'posh'. One informant commented: And some people could just be honest and say that looking like a fancy dish . . . yeah and somebody might be like "what really fancy about that?"' Another says: ' I don't know if she's trying to show what she cooked . . . making foh . . . focasi . . . foccacia' – probably it's something international, she's trying to be international, that kind of thing. Stush to me, if you stush you really ignorant with it. Some people have, like you could have stush clothes, stush food. That would definitely describe you as stush.' 'What's that you making there? Like people would put up a lot of things like "that looking real good gyurl" When in real, it's not looking good.' 'Because look at that. Tomatoes there? I don't really think it looking all that fancy. I think it looking like an omelette and they put tomatoes on top of it.' The one informant who does recognise it responds positively: 'She's experimental and confident in cooking. Brave enough to make something different.' More people, however, would just be confused as to what is going on.

Comparing across the nine sites of field work in the 'Why We Post' series, some show a tighter control over normativity than others. The clearest case of all would be the field site in North Chile.[4] Much of Haynes's book is concerned with how visual posts on Facebook show a pressure to post unpretentious, inclusive images that suppress differences in identity as well as in class. There, as noted in previous chapters within this book, the meme is a common instrument for establishing normativity.

As already noted, the normative can be bolstered by approval as well as disapproval. In Trinidad it is entirely acceptable to post a religious meme, while in The Glades some would see this as intrusive and an inappropriate presumption about other people's values and beliefs (Fig. 8.13). Trini informants responded that 'This picture just states the truth of what the scripture says' or 'You trying to spread the gospel as well. You really want people to understand your stance yes, and why there is a God'. Another reflected on the time it was posted: 'Yes, is a way to reinforce and to rise above all the Carnival mentality.... especially now for people who are church-going people, who are Christian people, who are religious and don't subscribe to the Carnival thing. They would more cleave at this thing at this time because we as a culture, we can get caught up in the Carnival thing.' This comment clearly reflects the dualism between the values of transience and transcendence discussed in Chapter 7.

Similarly the next image is one that would be unlikely to be posted in The Glades, but that has a clear and appropriate purpose for Trinidadians (Fig. 8.14). Trinidad is a country where births can elicit

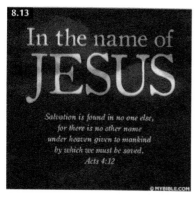

Religious meme

Couple showing pride in pregnancy

gossip over the likely paternity. However, this image reinforces a foundational principle of Trinidadian social relationships – the status of a man increases when a woman has his baby, while that of a woman increases when she has retained the affection of that baby's father. Informants recognised this and approved.

'I would be a little Trini right now and say – this is meh man, this is he child and this is meh child father.' Another states: ' yeah, this is my man, this is my child father, we having a baby together. She might go to the extent to say "all haters", because she might know it must be have some women like him. And as I saying she might go to an extent to say "all the haters go ahead and hate." [D: 'So haters just mean like people who are jealous of me?' I: 'Yeah, jealous people that, as the slang they use, – fight you down, bad mind.... So she know that it have some people don't want them to be together'.] Mostly, however, the comments are positive such as ' nice pregnancy pic.' or 'I'm proud of my girl, I'm proud that I'm gonna be a father', or 'She looks very happy...he look kinda neutral...but that's a man thing too...just being himself...as they would call it'. 'OK, that's definitely a proud couple and they expecting an...it have a baby in there.... a bun in the oven, yeah.'

How men succeed

So far the emphasis has been on understanding how critical responses help us to understand the mechanisms and pressures that create normative behaviour. But this book and the other 10 volumes are published under the title 'Why We Post', and in this last section we will show one rather different reason that explains why some people post what they post. This reason is simply that the right post can advance the interests of the person posting. To demonstrate this, we will use the example of posts that men use to seduce women.

Post claiming to show proper male sensibility

Most women who responded to this post took it at face value (Fig. 8.15). They assumed this was the sentiment that the person posting believed in. For example: 'A picture like this would say a lot of things. It would also say what type of person it is. It could be a Christian, as some Christians decide to really wait on God to send the right person for them. It could also be a non-Christian also because it have non-Christians who also decide to really wait as you read there. So I think somebody just post it after a bad experience or that's what they're feeling or maybe they hear a song that speaks about that and they decide to post it.'

For this reason, woman also tended to assume that it was a woman that had posted this meme. 'I think it's most likely a woman posting this. Well, from my experience, women mostly share those kinds of sentiments. Men really wouldn't share that. It could be directed to one particular person. Yes it could be, from my own experience, from my own use of Facebook. Yes, just posting it in terms of wanting to send a message to someone she loves or wants back. In terms of how we have begun to think, in terms of communicating, it's sort of the verbalisation of your love for the individual in a public space. So while it's a personal act, it has become a public thing. Yes, my friends would post things like this. I have posted things like this.' Another woman stated: 'Yeah, it is, I think it would be a woman posting. Yeah, I don't know if men would actually take the time to reflect on things like these, might be a woman. For the person to see, and if she is single, maybe it might give her a sense of justification for being single.' A third woman stated strongly: 'That is a woman post! I feel the woman – no honestly, it's kind of hard to see a guy post something so sentimental.' A final example of a woman commenting is less certain as to the poster's gender, but still assumes sincerity: 'Man or woman could post something like this because relationship is something that…you know…it could be a lot of things. It could be to get something out or it could be to encourage some person because you know in daily life, everyone experience different things during the day and by posting a certain post it could impact someone's life. It could be to one person, as I said they might have a bad experience, a break up, and they now come out of a relationship, and they just decide to post that to either get back at the person.'

Yet the evidence of our research was that men do routinely post memes of this kind, and the reason they do so was made brutally clear once we turned from the female to the male respondents. 'Women would suck up things like this. They like this kind of romantic things.' [D: 'OK. But some men would post it just to play they are sensitive and that kind of thing?' I: 'Yeah to rope in girls.' D: 'And girls would kind of believe it?' I: 'Not kind of – they will.' D: 'They will?' I: 'Yeah.' D: 'So this kind of thing does work?' I: 'Yeah.' Another man, as soon as the meme came up, responded: 'OK – we post things like this on our pages for "likes".' After hearing the different responses of the two genders, Danny then asked a woman whether, if a man had posted it, he would succeed in such a cynical aim. Her response was simply 'It would be successful'.

It's easy to take off your clothes and have sex; people do it all the time, but opening up your soul to someone, letting them into your spirit, thoughts, fears, future, hopes, and dreams... that's being naked.

Like Comment Share

Post about gender relations

The men seem clear that they use Facebook posting to take advantage of what they regard as women's gullibility in allowing them to pretend to an empathy that is merely a strategy for getting to sleep with more women. In the next case, the man posting seems to be getting the best of both worlds: he has the potential to both look sensitive and post something he would see as very sexy (Fig. 8.16). This is exactly what male informants saw: 'Yeah, well he's trying to show well...he's coming off in the way that every girl wants – a prince. I don't want you just for sex. I want to be with you. But the bottom line is they want sex. So he just not going directly. He just going around in a circle.' D: 'OK, and most men would do that?' I: 'All men do this.' Another male replied to Danny as follows: D: 'You think a guy would post this?' I: 'Yeah.' D: 'You think he's posting it because it's what he really thinks or...?' I: 'Reverse psychology.' D: 'You think he's using psychology. You think this would work out for him?' I: 'Yeah.'

By contrast, most women continued to take this as sincere. One suggested: 'Yeah, that's deep and it makes sense. It's about being naked and this is what being naked is. It's showing them yourself and the person is in a way venting. Maybe they're hurt and they just letting you know it. Like opening up your soul to someone. That is very deep.' Another said: 'I don't see men expressing these sentiments. I think a woman would be comfortable posting this because the nudity is not raw. It's not savage. It's not a woman with her breasts displayed, yuh know. So it's done very subtle in terms of how it's communicated. So you just see the outline of someone's side and a thumb slipping into the underwear. So it's not overt, it's not dirty, yeah.' A third stated: 'Its anti-sexual, I don't think it have much, because they use the sex as an example – but the main thing they say is that being naked is like you surrender, you open, you show that, well come into me. You naked. So it could be a lot of things, like spiritual being naked, a lot of things.' A fourth said, 'I know a guy who might post this'. D: 'For good reason or bad?' I: 'For...he's the emotional type, so he would just post it for posting it.' Finally, however, one woman did, on this occasion, see an alternative interpretation: 'If it was a man posting, I think it's not really his true feelings. Often you would find posts like this, like you would find fellas posting this, that girls would think they have a soft side and like them.'[5]

8.17

When a guy calls you hot,
he's looking at your body.
When a guy calls you pretty,
he's looking at your face.
When a guy calls you beautiful,
he's looking at your heart.

All three guys still wanna fuck you, though.

Post about true male intentions

By the stage of this final posting it might have seemed that there was no room left for ambiguity, given that it seems just to make explicit what these male informants were consistently stating. Yet even this posting elicited quite a variety of responses (Fig. 8.17). In this case, it was one of the men who assumed precisely because it was so open it must be a woman posting. 'OK... yeah, is a woman put that, a woman, definitely a woman. It just telling you the rawness of the male species... we just looking for action.' D: 'You think this is fairly true for Trini males?' I: 'In a general sense, yeah'. Women also saw this as a positive posting by a woman: 'I guess that's part of what would be empowering, these messages on Facebook that people put out as to, yuh know, yuh have a lot of those online yuh know, those empowerment messages where women share and re-post, and all of that. These things about being a strong woman, it's like feminism and social media.'

Some women still followed the logic of their previous responses, but this time realising that it led to a rather different conclusion. 'This one might be a male posting it, but a sensitive male. I would actually think that he wants to give the air of being sensitive and kind so that he can attract women. I think that's the way it normally is. Yeah sometimes to show females, "I'm considerate and I'm kind and I'm loving". Yuh know, when they're actually the total opposite.' As in the previous two cases, men could be a good deal more forthright about what was going on. D: 'You think it's put out for entertaining or like serious?' I: 'Nah I don't think it's serious. It's just like for a laugh.'

We would not wish to preclude the possibility that there are sensitive men who post such memes for sincere reasons, but the male respondents in this exercise do precisely refute such a possibility. For them, such memes are simply part of the strategic arsenal that men store up for the sole purpose of sleeping with more women, pretty much exactly the sentiment of the final meme.

Conclusion

It may seem asymmetrical to have not conducted the same exercise in The Glades, but we found this would just not have been possible. There are contexts in which people in The Glades enjoy banter and putting other people down, such as at the pub or at school. But when asked to look at other people's postings they were generally cautious, reticent and mainly polite. In our ethnography at El Mirador, we had already seen people enjoying collective dissection of other peoples' Facebook profiles, so this seemed quite a natural thing to do. However, in The Glades it would have seemed forced and made people uncomfortable.

Yet in the preceding chapters, it is the English in The Glades who if anything seem more homogeneous and conformist, suggesting a still greater pressure to normativity. The reason is that people in England achieve the same effect using different means. Instead of this explicit talking, we have in fact already encountered the analogous behaviour in The Glades when we examined their use of humour online. The one place where the English seem quite unrestricted is in funny postings, indeed the word 'fuck' probably appears a good deal more often in The Glades postings than in El Mirador. In England one can get away with many more things as long as they are considered funny.

In both societies, people have differing expectations about how an individual should respond to such criticism. Trinidadians have their own pride in their ability to take negative comments as funny and not serious. One of the worst things a Trinidadian can do is to lose their temper and self-control, actions described as being 'ignorant'. A true Trini always keeps things on the surface as humour and banter to show that they can 'take it'. By contrast, central to individual sensibility in The Glades are self-deprecation and irony, both of which are rarely found in postings within El Mirador. So each place has its own normative ways of creating and responding to critical pressures – which explains why this exercise worked very well in Trinidad, but would have been inappropriate for The Glades.

It seemed worthwhile to avail ourselves of this opportunity within Trinidad simply because this chapter plays such an important role in explaining the content of others. The topic of this book is, after all, social media – it is the anticipated responses of other people to one's postings which explains the patterns of posting that we have found, as well as the pressures and constraints that emerge as each society's values often contrast with those of the other. These are the processes that help us to understand typicality and normativity in both field sites.

9
Conclusion

We began this book with several aims in mind. The most obvious was simply an acknowledgement that in the past books have emphasised the textual over the visual. This was largely for technical and financial reasons. Books and journal articles with many colour images were expensive both to print and purchase. We have been slow to recognise the bias this may have led to. Our aim was to give these visual posts their due both in terms of attention and replication, properly reflecting the degree to which photos and memes now dominate the social media posts of some regions.

The second point was to demonstrate the potential of comparative anthropology. As papers start to emerge by anthropologists about visual postings on social media around the world,[1] it becomes obvious that these may vary considerably from place to place. This is very evident throughout the entire 'Why We Post' set of publications dealing with nine different field sites. But this may be the first book that attempts a systematic comparison including both qualitative and quantitative evidence to show just how different such visual postings may be. Our third aim comes from the task of explaining these differences. Could such material have the potential for the kind of anthropological analysis of culture and values that we would have previously attempted using more conventional ethnography?

Ethnography is concerned with patterns and trends rather than the individual, distinguishing us from, for example, psychology. It differs from journalism in that our main interest is the typical and general rather than the sensational or exceptional. The many examples of both a quantitative and qualitative difference between our two field sites brings us to a concern with typicality. We have tried to be careful in not claiming that The Glades 'is' England or El Mirador 'is' Trinidad. We have given constant reminders that there is variation, based not only on sociological parameters such as class and ethnicity, but also always at the level of individual preferences. At the same time we acknowledge that both populations themselves engage in constant discussion as to the nature of Trinidadian and English culture and behaviour, which clearly influences and resonates with our own generalisations.

The early chapters give a sense of people being socialised into certain expectations and norms as they grow up. By Chapter 7, this allows us to consider the basic values which are being expressed in the two field sites. In the case of Trinidad, this corresponded closely with Miller's earlier ethnographic study, published as *Modernity: An Ethnographic Approach*.[2] There he suggested that Trinidadian values have developed in a 'dualist' mode resulting from the specific history of the island, whose population consists largely of descendants from either enslaved Africans or indentured East Indians. In that book, Miller argued that this radical rupture from their place of origin led people to develop two opposing projects. On the one hand there is a quite systematic attempt to embody a sense of freedom, which is transient and individual and expressed through events such as carnival and idioms such as sexuality. Things should be kept on the surface rather than institutionalised, which would have made them a possible focus of hierarchy and oppression. On the other hand there is a desire to reconstruct a sense of missing roots, expressed through a concern with extended family and an orientation to the longer term. Such values include gaining substance through education, respecting the home and tradition, and showing a strong commitment to religion.

In turn, this leads us to re-think the three contradictory factors analysed in Chapter 5 of this book.[3] We see through inspection of these visual posts that there are parallels between the distinctions of gender, of ethnicity and of class in Trinidad, which are not independent of each other. Transience as an expression of freedom may become the burden of males, but also of Afro-Trinidadians and of the lower-income population. Meanwhile the need to re-construct roots and focus on the longer term may become the burden of females, but also of Indo-Trinidadians and the higher-income populations. What this means is that the basic dualism of Trinidadian values is made clear by projecting them onto categories of people – and then repeating that dualism for three different contrasts between social groups.

This is a characteristic of anthropological analysis. Most anthropology consists of cultural generalisations, which can be confused with stereotypes. The difference between the two is called essentialism. Essentialism means that cultural behaviour is an inherent property of that population, related to their biology, psychology or some essential feature. By contrast, anthropology accepts that culture is normative and that we can describe peoples' behaviour as 'typical', but our analysis is used to find the reasons behind that behaviour, which are usually historical and cultural. We thereby demonstrate how, under other circumstances, these people's values and behaviours could have been entirely different. When we see these parallels between class, gender and ethnicity we realise that these are simply distinctions that are being exploited by cultural values and projected on to people. They are not an inherent condition of being female, or Indo-Trinidadian, or of high income.

From this perspective, we are not free agents who determine our own values: rather we are more like objects, things that carry the values of culture. We don't just post memes. By being ourselves a devout Christian or a devotee of hip-hop we are as individuals also a kind of meme: people who embody, express and thereby share Christianity or hip-hop culture. The contrast doesn't have to be between categories such as males verses females. It could equally well be the contrast between Carnival as a celebration of freedom and Christmas as a celebration of tradition. Furthermore, in Chapter 7 we found that in El Mirador this was not just a contrast between different peoples. The core dualism of transience and transcendence also emerged as a contrast *within the postings* of the same individuals. The same people seem happy to post some visuals that are strongly religious, moral and nationalistic, but simultaneously other posts which are highly sexualised and transgressive.

The historical reasons behind this dualism in Trinidadian values derive from slavery and indentured labour. This is very different from the history of the English people who live in The Glades. However, there may again be deep historical factors that account for the patterns that we discovered and analysed in Chapter 6. The first posts to be analysed in that chapter consisted of photographs of pet dogs and cats, and the visual material made clear the association between these pets and children. According to the historian Keith Thomas,[4] this association, and in some cases substitution, between pets and children had become well established by the sixteenth century; it may have begun even earlier. The anthropologist Alan Macfarlane[5] has also shown how this and much other evidence speaks to an unusual and early sense of the individualism of children and people more generally in England. In turn, this rebounded upon our views of 'nature' and may contribute to the development of a cosmology which we now find embodied in the suburban ideals that are the substance of much of the rest of that chapter.

As a result the people of The Glades, for the most part, eschew the projects of transience and transcendence that dominate the postings of the people of El Mirador. They avoid most of the overt sexualisation and emphasis on the cultivation of the appearance of individuals on the one hand, but have far fewer religious, nationalistic and overt statements of tradition and social identity on the other. Rather they seek a moderation and self-effacement that helps them to occupy this middle ground of the suburban middle class. Both as persons and through the objects around them, including properties and pets, they define a set of cultural values quite precisely by a systematic opposition to the two ends of the spectrum of values. There are also some internal oppositions, such as a strong contrast between males and female posting in certain areas and as seen in through a rather repressed but still present culture of working-class values that are determinedly opposed to those of the dominant factions of this society. So in their own way, the values of the English are just as expressive as those of Trinidad. Particular mechanisms, such as humour, are used to control and patrol the boundaries, and to denigrate those who have pretensions that might threaten them.

This is another major finding of this book. If anthropology depends upon people largely conforming to what are seen as appropriate images and avoiding those regarded as inappropriate, then this normativity, this moral order, must be reproduced through some device that keeps people largely in line. The point of Chapter 8 was to present our evidence for how precisely this happens. By asking people to comment on visual images posted by people they don't know, our informants had licence to express what were often scathing condemnations and sarcastic denigrations of every element of an image that they felt crossed their lines of normativity. We did not repeat this experiment for the English people of The Glades since they tend to be more circumspect, so the material would probably have been less rich. But the very evidence for the consistency and reticence in what they actually post speaks volumes for the degree to which the English are as controlling over cultural norms as people from Trinidad.

Chapter 8 then serves another role. The very structure of the book and its levels of generality lead us internally to homogenise these two populations. At the same time there are, of course, individuals in both sites who are highly creative, enjoy repudiating all such pressures and conventions and will look exceptional. Chapter 8 also shows that individuals may have very different and quite contrasting interpretations of the same photograph. No image in this book has a single meaning outside of this spectrum of interpretations to which it is subject by all those who view it. The point is to keep these things in balance. The term 'Trini' should not preclude an acknowledgement of the individualism and diversity of particular Trinidadians, many of whom are very particular. But a focus only on individual difference would equally preclude the evidence for generalisation and typicality that emerges just as strongly from our evidence.

The decision to conduct systematic reviews of 50 profiles in each field site, which meant examining up to 30,000 images, was partly intended to balance any potential accusation that we have selected material merely to suit a given argument. These quantitative surveys were used to support the arguments for difference, though in the introduction we acknowledged that quantitative studies do not preclude qualitative elements. For example, if we take the overall mass of photos, we find that Trinidadian women are more than twice as likely to post images of themselves alone as are those of The Glades (1,006 as against 415), and far more likely to try and look 'hot' than those in The Glades (354 as against 52). All of this supports the discussion in Chapter 7.

These surveys provide a mid-level between grand generalisations about El Mirador and The Glades and a concern to acknowledge individual difference. We see all sorts of partial generalisations about particular groups within each field site – things that many or most but rarely all people in that group do; difference may be quite pronounced or not very pronounced at all. In The Glades, for instance, middle-aged and older adults are more likely to post on issues of the environment or climate change, while in El Mirador this would be more common among younger people. In The Glades, females are as likely as males to post about science or IT, while in El Mirador the majority of such posts are from males. In The Glades women seem almost entirely to subsume themselves under the portrayal of their children in visual posts, while in El Mirador the posts of mothers retain a stronger sense of their own identity. One complication is that comparison involved various parameters – for example, age can complicate factors of both gender and region. Sometimes a gender distinction such as females posting more profile pictures than males is true for both younger and older people, but sometimes the more significant reason for difference seems to be age itself. While we conduct surveys and make simple comparisons of the incidence of categories or photographs, we do not use the language of 'samples' or 'correlations'. These would give a false objectivity to our findings, which might well have been rather different in the next village or the next year. We cannot escape the burden of interpretation that relies on a vast amount of knowledge that is not quantifiable – nor should we want to.

We fully acknowledge that there are many arenas which are not especially contrastive. Browsing through the Appendix reveals all sorts of similarities between the two sites as well as striking contrasts. It would be astonishing if there were not these many cases of similarity. The very specific elements of Facebook, such as the use of walls or 'likes', are common simply because the platform contrasts with some earlier social media, for example MySpace, in being rather more controlling of how it is used. People in The Glades and El Mirador have taken equally to the sharing of memes. They also share many of the same jokes, videos and sensationalist news. A series of memes such as 'Keep Calm' or a viral phenomenon such as the 'Harlem Shake' demonstrates its global reach by appearing in both regions. Many Trinidadians have relatives in England; on one occasion when he was working as a volunteer for a church tea, Miller was flabbergasted to discover that one of the other volunteers was actually a Trinidadian born in El Mirador and now living in The Glades. As they say – what were the chances? There is so much common culture, ranging from centuries of colonial rule and education to more recent global media, from Beyoncé to *Game of Thrones*. So Facebook both homogenises a bit and reflects prior commonalities quite a lot. If this volume has emphasised cultural difference, it is mainly because that is the more neglected side of the evidence – and because, given the factors just outlined, the retention and development of new contrasts seemed impressive. People also often extrapolate from the common material to assume an entirely homogenised world. This volume shows us a very different picture.

In refuting the idea that social media is contributing to cultural homogenisation, we also contest its sibling argument that every modern development represents something called a loss of culture. The people of The Glades are no more and no less cultural than those of El Mirador and no more or less than their ancestors of several centuries ago. The young are no more or less cultural than the old. It is just a question of the respect paid by anthropologists to people's everyday lives, and a general willingness to see patterns of contemporary culture as emanations of deep historical and cosmological issues – concepts which to us as anthropologists seem very evident. Yes, people trade apparently thoughtless and inconsequential postings that litter modern social media, leading to the current critique of the selfie or the castigation of such postings as the 'dross' of day-to-day life. These are often taken as a sign of our growing superficiality, in comparison with some nostalgia-drenched past. But prior to social media, the people of El Mirador or The Glades who met face to face in the street were equally likely to have been gossiping about their friends or discussing the weather, not debating philosophy.

The final joy of writing this particular book compared to previous volumes is simply that the topic was visual postings, giving us a wonderful opportunity literally to *show* what we mean. In other papers, we will examine more analytically the transformations in photography that make social media photographs in some ways an unprecedented phenomenon.[6] This book is both a reflection and acknowledgement of the fact that people now post images online in their billions every day. As a result, photography's traditional aims of memorialisation and representation have now been complemented by an additional concern: it is a major aspect of everyday communication, which on social media rivals that of voice and text.

The visual postings on Facebook do not represent all the visual postings in The Glades. In contrast to in El Mirador, by 2014 other platforms such as Twitter, Instagram and Snapchat had for young people already become at least as important as Facebook, if not more so, as a place to post images. In *Social Media in an English Village,*[7] Chapter 3 provides an analysis of the contrasts and similarities between young people's postings on Twitter and Instagram that complements the evidence of this book. So we cannot pretend the materials presented in this book are even representative of visual postings on social media, let alone of the myriad other ways in which people express themselves.

So we do not claim that this volume is comprehensive in any respect. Yet we hope that we have demonstrated how much is to be gained by welcoming with open arms this new visibility in the world. Photographs have been around for a long time. But this new, comparatively costless and effortless technology of camera phones, which enables images to be posted to a social media platform in seconds, is unprecedented. A large proportion of the people of our world thereby not only have a new visual language, they have recourse to a vast ocean of visual images, either being shared as memes or newly taken by individuals. This book itself represents a snapshot of this historical moment of visual enlightenment, in which the world is just starting to explore the potential of such visual display. It is as though we were living through the invention of clothing as an expressive form. We hope that we have contributed to this acknowledgement, but we finish with a sense that so much more can, and will, be learnt from these developments.

Appendix

We balanced our qualitative ethnographic study with quantitative surveys. In brief, each of us selected 50 of our informants' profiles divided into four categories: 1) school pupils/young people, 2) those that had finished education but were not yet parents, 3) parents of young children, and finally 4) those with adult children or older people without children. In each category we took equal numbers of male and female informants. The only difference is that Miller has 20 informants who were school pupils aged 16–18 while Sinanan has 15 school pupils with a greater age spread. In our sample people first joined Facebook as follows:

	The Glades	El Mirador
2006	1	2
2007	18	5
2008	9	17
2009	16	12
2010	2	6
2011	0	4
2012	1	2
2013	1	0
2014	0	2

The postings of these 100 informants are presented in relation to four types of analysis. Figure 1 is based on the most recent 150 of the photos they have posted themselves and the most recent 150 of their tagged photos. The total is less than 30,000 since some informants had far fewer than 300 photos on the site. Nevertheless, this book is based on the examination of at least 20,000 photographs, though the total photos posted by this sample is nearly 60,000 since most had more than 300 photos. Figure 2 is a survey of all the 'Profile Pictures' on the Facebook walls of these 100 selected informants. Figure 3 is an analysis of all the photos that we deemed to be selfies, meaning self-taken through a